D1468762

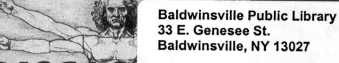

DISEASES & DISORDERS

Cervical Cancer

Kris Hirschmann

LUCENT BOOKS
A part of Gale, Cengage Learning

GALE
CENGAGE Learning

Detroit • New York • San Francisco • New Haven, Conn • Waterville, Maine • London

GALE
CENGAGE Learning™

JUL 1 6 2010

© 2010 Gale, Cengage Learning

LIBRARY OF CONGRESS CATALOGING-IN-PUBLICATION DATA

Hirschmann, Kris, 1967-
  Cervical cancer / by Kris Hirschmann.
    p. cm. -- (Diseases and disorders)
  Includes bibliographical references and index.
  ISBN 978-1-4205-0216-9 (hardcover)
  1. Cervix uteri--Cancer--Popular works. I. Title.
  RC280.U8H57 2010
  616.99'466--dc22

                                        2009043795

Lucent Books
27500 Drake Rd.
Farmington Hills, MI 48331

ISBN-13: 978-1-4205-0216-9
ISBN-10: 1-4205-0216-6

Printed in the United States of America
1 2 3 4 5 6 7 14 13 12 11 10

Printed by Bang Printing, Brainerd, MN, 1st Ptg., 02/2010

Table of Contents

"The Most Difficult Puzzles Ever Devised"

Charles Best, one of the pioneers in the search for a cure for diabetes, once explained what it is about medical research that intrigued him so. "It's not just the gratification of knowing one is helping people," he confided, "although that probably is a more heroic and selfless motivation. Those feelings may enter in, but truly, what I find best is the feeling of going toe to toe with nature, of trying to solve the most difficult puzzles ever devised. The answers are there somewhere, those keys that will solve the puzzle and make the patient well. But how will those keys be found?"

Since the dawn of civilization, nothing has so puzzled people—and often frightened them, as well—as the onset of illness in a body or mind that had seemed healthy before. A seizure, the inability of a heart to pump, the sudden deterioration of muscle tone in a small child—being unable to reverse such conditions or even to understand why they occur was unspeakably frustrating to healers. Even before there were names for such conditions, even before they were understood at all, each was a reminder of how complex the human body was, and how vulnerable.

While our grappling with understanding diseases has been frustrating at times, it has also provided some of humankind's most heroic accomplishments. Alexander Fleming's accidental discovery in 1928 of a mold that could be turned into penicillin has resulted in the saving of untold millions of lives. The isolation of the enzyme insulin has reversed what was once a death sentence for anyone with diabetes. There have been great strides in combating conditions for which there is not yet a cure, too. Medicines can help AIDS patients live longer, diagnostic tools such as mammography and ultrasounds can help doctors find tumors while they are treatable, and laser surgery techniques have made the most intricate, minute operations routine.

This "toe-to-toe" competition with diseases and disorders is even more remarkable when seen in a historical continuum. An astonishing amount of progress has been made in a very short time. Just two hundred years ago, the existence of germs as a cause of some diseases was unknown. In fact, it was less than 150 years ago that a British surgeon named Joseph Lister had difficulty persuading his fellow doctors that washing their hands before delivering a baby might increase the chances of a healthy delivery (especially if they had just attended to a diseased patient)!

Each book in Lucent's Diseases and Disorders series explores a disease or disorder and the knowledge that has been accumulated (or discarded) by doctors through the years. Each book also examines the tools used for pinpointing a diagnosis, as well as the various means that are used to treat or cure a disease. Finally, new ideas are presented—techniques or medicines that may be on the horizon.

Frustration and disappointment are still part of medicine, for not every disease or condition can be cured or prevented. But the limitations of knowledge are being pushed outward constantly; the "most difficult puzzles ever devised" are finding challengers every day.

A Preventable Plague

"**I**'m very sorry, but the test results show that you have cervical cancer."

Each year, doctors around the world deliver this news to nearly half a million women. For some of these patients the prognosis is good. The cancer was caught early and will be easy to treat. For others the situation is much more dire: The cancer has reached an advanced stage. Treatment will be long and difficult, and in the end it may fail. More than half of all cervical cancer victims die as a result of their disorder.

This statistic is deeply disturbing to most doctors. Health officials point out that cervical cancer is among the easiest cancers to prevent, detect, and treat. Under ideal circumstances it would kill almost no one. But sadly, circumstances today are not ideal. Many women, especially those in poor nations, cannot or do not receive regular gynecological checkups. The early warning signs of cervical cancer, therefore, go undetected. By the time noticeable symptoms appear, the disorder has often progressed too far to be treated effectively.

This situation may improve. Recently developed treatments and vaccines are giving health care providers new tools in the fight against cervical cancer. Additionally, public education efforts in less-developed areas are encouraging women to take better care of their reproductive health. The combination of better health care and increased awareness should lead to a dramatic decrease in cervical cancer deaths.

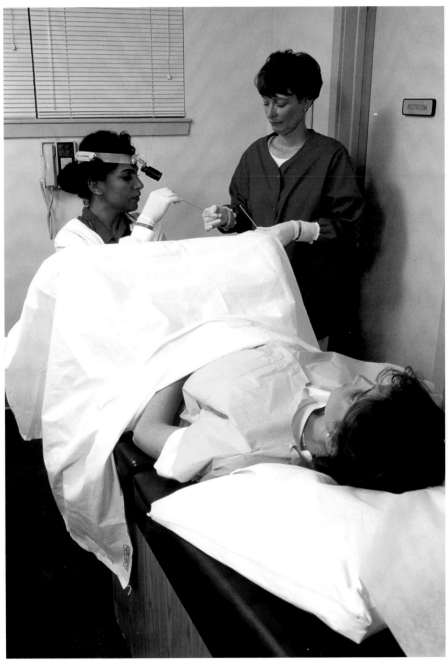

In undeveloped countries women often ignore the early warning signs of cervical cancer because they do not have access to gynecological exams.

But will it?

Some health officials are doubtful. They worry that it will be very hard to provide proper care in poor nations, where women need it most. In these places, issues of cost and culture create barriers that will be difficult to overcome.

Difficult, yes—but perhaps not impossible. Many scientists believe that the world health community is ready and able to tackle this challenge. As scientist Juliet V. Spencer puts it, "We currently have all the tools needed to eliminate this health problem. . . . If cervical cancer continues to kill women 50 years from now, it will be because not enough attention was paid and insufficient energy expended to stop the pain and suffering."[1]

With these words, Spencer lays a heavy responsibility upon the global health care network and upon women everywhere. Governments and health organizations must provide the resources to prevent and detect cervical cancer. Women must educate themselves and take the appropriate steps to keep themselves healthy. By working together, doctors and patients in even the most disadvantaged areas can conquer the cervical cancer plague.

CHAPTER ONE

What Is Cervical Cancer?

Cancer is a disorder that occurs when a cell's DNA, or genetic information, is damaged. When the damaged cell reproduces, its offspring cells are not quite normal. They may look or act differently from their undamaged neighbors. Sometimes they are able to reproduce in ways that the body does not normally allow. When this is the case, the mutated cells may start whole colonies of cells just like themselves.

Mutant colonies come in two types. The first type grows as a group, creating a tumor that does not branch into the surrounding tissues. Noninvasive tumors are called benign. The second type of colony infects and invades anything it touches. Invasive tumors are called cancerous growths, malignancies, or simply cancer.

Cancer can develop in almost any part of the human body. A cancer is usually named after the area or organ it affects. Cervical cancer, thus, is cancer that develops in the tissues of the cervix. Since only women have cervixes, cervical cancer is strictly a women's disorder.

On a global scale, cervical cancer is a major health threat. It is the fifth most common cancer in women (after breast, lung, stomach, and colorectal cancer). In 2002 (the most recent year for which data are available) the International

Agency for Research on Cancer (IARC) reported 493,243 new cases of this disorder. During the same year a reported 273,505 women—about 55 percent of those affected—died from cervical cancer.

The Female Reproductive System

The cervix is part of the female reproductive system. A female's reproductive organs are located inside the lower abdomen. The main organ of the reproductive system is the uterus, which is sometimes also called the womb. Most of the time the uterus is hollow and pear shaped. During pregnancy it holds the developing fetus or fetuses. Its elastic walls stretch as needed to accommodate the unborn offspring.

Several passages lead into or out of the uterus. Two upper passages connect to the fallopian tubes, each of which leads to a round organ called an ovary. The ovaries contain the female reproductive cells, which are called ova or eggs. Each month, the ovaries release one or more eggs. The eggs travel downward through the fallopian tubes, where they may be fertilized if they encounter sperm (male reproductive cells). Fertilized eggs eventually reach the uterus, where they implant themselves in the uterine wall and start developing into fetuses.

Unfertilized eggs also reach the uterus, but they do not remain there. Along with any unneeded uterine lining, these cells are flushed from the body as part of a woman's monthly menstrual cycle. They exit the uterus by passing through the cervix (which is part of the uterus) into the vagina. The vagina is a fleshy tube about the length of an adult's finger. Open to the external environment, it allows fluids and tissues to leave the body and other objects (such as sanitary products, medical instruments, or the male penis during sexual intercourse) to enter.

Structure and Function of the Cervix

The cervix itself is long and narrow. It is sometimes referred to as the neck of the uterus. The lower part of the neck juts into the upper region of the vagina. About 1 inch (2.5cm) long and 1 inch wide, this structure is called the ectocervix. It is sometimes also called the exocervix.

Female Reproductive System

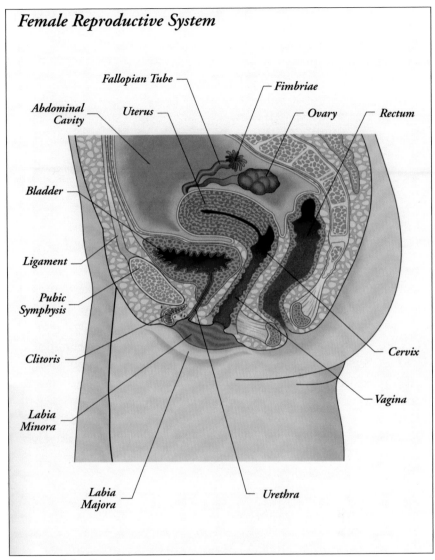

View of the female reproductive system.

The ectocervix has a central opening called the external os. (*Os* is the Latin term for "mouth.") This opening leads into a passage called the endocervical canal, which runs the length of the cervix. It ends at the uterine cavity with another opening called the internal os.

The cervix is not merely a channel between the uterine cavity and the vagina. It is also the uterus's gatekeeper, allowing only certain things to enter or leave the body. The cervix secretes a thick mucus, for instance, that blocks bacteria and other harmful organisms from entering the uterus. It thins this mucus each month during ovulation to let sperm enter. The cervix clamps shut during pregnancy to protect the fetus and keep it securely in the womb and then stretches wide during labor and delivery to release the fully developed baby. It also stretches to let menstrual materials leave the body. Between all these jobs, the cervix plays an important role in a woman's reproductive health and everyday well-being.

Cells of the Cervix

Cancer starts with a single abnormal cell. In the cervix these abnormalities tend to occur in the cells that cover the cervical surface, or the epithelium. These cells are called epithelial cells.

The surface of the cervix has two types of epithelial cells. The cells that cover the ectocervix are called squamous epithelial cells. They are large and hexagonal in shape. They lie on top of each other in multiple layers, creating a thick barrier that blocks infectious agents. Additionally, the uppermost squamous cells contain a material called keratin. This is the same material that forms human hair and fingernails. It makes the cells hard and extremely resistant to infection.

The cells that line the endocervical canal are called columnar epithelial cells or sometimes glandular cells. These cells are tall and thin, and they occur in a single layer. They do not contain keratin, so they are much softer than the squamous cells of the ectocervix.

The region where columnar cells give way to squamous cells is called the transformation zone, or sometimes the transition zone. It is often dubbed the TZ for short. In this area, an abrupt change occurs from one type of cell to another. The squamous cells of the TZ are newer, softer, and less protected than the better-established cells on the ectocervix. For this reason, the TZ is especially vulnerable to attack by infectious agents.

Female Reproductive Cancers

Cancer can affect any part of the female reproductive system. After the cervix, the ovaries are the most commonly affected area. Over 200,000 new cases of ovarian cancer are diagnosed worldwide each year. More than half of all ovarian cancer victims eventually die from the disorder.

Cancer of the uterus is another serious problem. Like ovarian cancer, this disorder strikes about 200,000 women each year. However, it has a much better cure rate. About 75 percent of the women who develop uterine cancer recover fully, with treatment.

Cancer of the vulva (the exterior parts of the female reproductive system) and the vagina can also occur. These conditions are much less common than other reproductive cancers. Worldwide statistics are not kept for these disorders. But in 2005 (the most recent year for which figures are available) about 6,000 new cases of vulvar and vaginal cancer were diagnosed in the United States alone.

Cancer of the uterus is located on the cervix or the body of the uterus. It is just one of many cancers that attack the reproductive system.

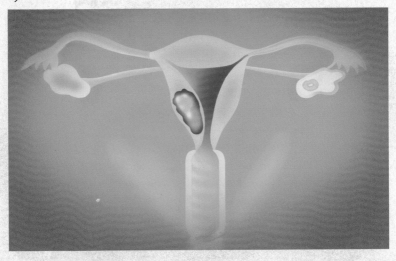

The size and location of the TZ change along with a woman's age. In preadolescent girls columnar cells extend onto the ecto-cervix. The TZ is, therefore, found on the ectocervix as well. During puberty, however, the body begins to prepare a girl for sexual intercourse by hardening the skin of the ectocervix. It does this by replacing columnar cells with tougher, keratin-loaded squamous cells. As time goes by, the area of columnar cells retreats farther and farther into the endocervical canal. Accordingly, the transformation zone shifts inward as well. In mature women the TZ may disappear entirely into the endocervical canal.

Physician and writer Shobha S. Krishnan makes an interesting point about this process. Because the tender TZ is more exposed in teens, she says, "Young adolescent women are especially more susceptible to . . . sexually transmitted infections."[2] As a result, girls who have sex at an early age are more likely than older women to contract cervical infections. These infections may lead to more serious conditions, up to and including cervical cancer.

Cervical Dysplasia

In a normal cervix the squamous cells lie in organized layers. The bottom layers (those farthest from the skin's surface) are made of young, round cells. The middle layers are made of older, somewhat flattened cells. The upper layer consists of the oldest cells, which have become very flat and hard.

In an abnormal cervix this pattern is disrupted. Disrupted growth is called cervical dysplasia, from the Latin words *dys*, meaning "abnormal," and *plasia*, or "growth." It may also be called cervical intraepithelial neoplasia, or CIN. *Neo* is Latin for "new," so this term translates roughly to "cervical skin new growth."

Medical professionals recognize three levels of CIN. The first level, CIN I, is informally called mild dysplasia. This term means that only a few abnormal cells are present, and they spread through less than one-third of the thickness of the epithelium. None of the abnormal cells have broken through the bottom layer of the epithelium, which is called the basement membrane.

Mild dysplasia is a very common condition, affecting up to 1 million American women each year. It can appear at any age, but it is most common in women between twenty-five and thirty-five years old. It has no uncomfortable symptoms, and it often goes away on its own. For these reasons, doctors seldom treat mild dysplasia. They simply monitor the patient's condition to make sure it does not get any worse.

About 30 percent of mild dysplasias do progress to a more serious level. When this happens, they are classified as CIN II, or moderate dysplasia. In moderate dysplasia a larger number of abnormal cells are present. These cells affect up to two-thirds of the epithelium's thickness. As in CIN I, the basement membrane remains intact.

Like mild dysplasia, moderate dysplasia often cures itself. One study found that only 25 percent of moderate dysplasia cases got more serious over a five-year period. Few doctors, however, are willing to take a wait-and-see approach to this disorder. They will usually treat the condition to avoid any chance of complications.

The final level of dysplasia, CIN III, is informally called severe dysplasia. In this condition many or all of the epithelial cells appear abnormal, and the entire thickness of the cervical epithelium is disordered. The basement membrane still has not been broached, but it is definitely in trouble. It is thickly lined with mutated cells that will push into the underlying tissues if they get a chance.

Severe dysplasia is also called carcinoma in situ (CIS), which means "cancer in place." This term can be alarming to patients. On an Internet message board, a twenty-five-year-old woman named Millie expresses her feelings about this diagnosis: "The [test] results say I have cervical carcinoma in situ. . . . I am very confused, uncertain, and of course scared. . . . This is devastating."[3]

Millie and others in her position do not need to be so frightened. Because carcinoma in situ is contained in the epithelium, it is easy to remove. It is usually considered a precancerous condition rather than full-blown cancer. The condition must, however, be treated immediately and aggressively to stop it from progressing.

Cervical Cancer

Left alone, carcinoma in situ is likely to break through the epithelium's basement membrane. When it does, it is considered cancerous. It is formally called invasive carcinoma because it has invaded the deep tissues of the cervix.

Invasive cervical carcinoma has several types. The most common type is called squamous cell carcinoma. Accounting for 80 to 90 percent of all diagnoses, this condition arises in the cervix's squamous cells. It usually starts in the transformation zone, where the squamous cells are most vulnerable.

If invasive cervical carcinomas are undetected or undiagnosed they will spread to the uterus or other nearby organs, as shown in this X-ray.

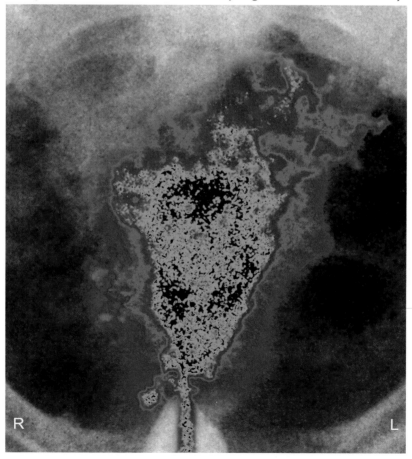

The second most common type of cervical cancer is called adenocarcinoma. This type of cancer develops deeper in the endocervical canal, in the cervix's columnar cells. It accounts for 10 to 20 percent of all diagnoses. Some studies have found that adenocarcinoma is harder to cure than squamous cell carcinoma. Other studies, however, have not found the same result, so this finding is controversial.

No one doubts the severity of small cell cervical cancer, a rare disorder that accounts for less than 3 percent of all diagnoses. Under a microscope the cells associated with this condition look small and round, with large, egg yolk–like centers. The cells multiply very quickly. Small cell cervical cancer may, therefore, develop into an extremely serious condition before it is detected. For this reason, and also because fast-spreading malignancies in general are hard to treat, the prognosis is poor for small cell cervical cancer patients.

Early cervical cancer has few symptoms. Many women, in fact, have no symptoms at all. Others experience light vaginal bleeding or cramping after sexual intercourse or when they are not having their menstrual periods. Post-menopausal women may notice these symptoms right away. Women of childbearing age, who expect to see vaginal blood from time to time, are more likely to ignore this early sign of cervical cancer.

One cervical cancer victim remembers the dangerous consequences of ignoring her symptoms. "I had been having a lot of bleeding and cramping for months before I even decided to go and see my doctor. I was diagnosed with a precancerous condition. I let it go for almost two years, and then I started having more pain and even heavier bleeding. . . . The easily treated precancer had turned into invasive cancer,"[4] she recalls.

The Cancer Spreads

Most invasive cervical carcinomas grow slowly. If they are caught early, they are fairly easy to cure. If cervical cancer goes undetected, however, the diseased cells continue to multiply. The malignancy spreads into new areas, getting larger and deadlier with each passing week.

The first affected area is the cervix itself. Cancerous cells invade the cervix's deep tissues. They creep outward and upward from their starting point, eventually transforming the entire cervix into a lumpy, cauliflower-like mass. At the same time, the infection spreads into the upper vagina. It also leaps into the tissues surrounding the vagina and the cervix.

From this point the cancer can go in many different directions. It may grow toward the pelvic sidewall, where it can block the tubes that drain urine from the kidneys to the bladder. It may spread into the bladder or the rectum. It may even grow into the abdominal cavity, where it starts new colonies of mutated cells. This spread is called metastasis, and it is an extremely serious situation.

The deadliest development occurs when cervical cancer breaks into either the bloodstream or the lymphatic system, a network of tubes that move fluids throughout the body. Either of these systems can carry cancerous cells to distant parts of the body. Once there, the cells may settle and start new colonies. Cervical cancer cells are most likely to settle in the lungs, liver, brain, or any combination of these organs. When they do, they keep multiplying, creating new malignancies and new sets of problems for the patient.

Patients with advanced cervical cancer are usually very uncomfortable. They often suffer from heavy vaginal bleeding and painful cramps in the pelvic area. In many women, the pain is especially bad during menstruation. A cervical cancer victim named Rena vividly remembers the menstrual period that finally drove her to the doctor. "It was so bad I can't even describe the pain. It felt like I was in hard labor for about eight days,"[5] she remembers.

Along with the pain, cervical cancer may also cause extreme weight loss and fatigue. Back pain, leg pain, swelling, and bone fractures sometimes occur. Localized symptoms in the brain, lungs, and other areas of metastasis also develop.

By the time a patient experiences these symptoms, she is in a dire situation. Riddled with cancer, she may also develop a life-threatening infection. Blood loss may lead to anemia, a condition in which the blood cannot carry enough oxygen to the organs. At the same time, blocked kidney drainage may force

Maria Eva Duarte de Perón (1919–1952)

Thanks to the musical *Evita*, the story of Maria Eva Duarte de Perón is familiar to people everywhere. Born to a poor family in rural Argentina, Eva moved to the nation's capital of Buenos Aires when she was just fifteen years old. She quickly became a star of stage, radio, and film. In 1945 she married a soldier named Juan Perón, who was elected president of Argentina the following year.

First Lady Eva, or "Evita" as she was more commonly called, was beloved by the people. She became so popular that she was invited to run for vice president in 1951. Evita declined the invitation, however, due to her failing health. Examinations revealed that she had developed an advanced case of cervical cancer. Doctors did their best for Evita, but it was not enough. The thirty-three-year-old icon died on July 26, 1952, becoming one of history's best-known and most tragic victims of cervical cancer.

urine and the poisons it carries to back up into the circulatory system. Any of these conditions will finally kill the patient.

Keeping the Killer at Bay

Many women die each year from cervical cancer. The good news, say doctors, is that this trend does not have to continue. Cervical dysplasias, including carcinoma in situ, are thought to have a 100 percent cure rate. This means that women who look after their reproductive health can stop potential problems before they get serious. With education, today's young women are unlikely to develop—let alone die from—cervical cancer.

CHAPTER TWO

What Causes Cervical Cancer?

Some types of cancer are mysterious, erupting for no clear reason. This is not the case with cervical cancer. Researchers have learned that this disorder develops after a woman is exposed to certain viruses called human papillomaviruses (HPVs). In the best-known study of this link, 997 out of 1,000 cervical cancer patients were found to carry dangerous forms of HPV. It is likely that the other three patients carried the virus as well, at levels too low for tests to detect. "Our studies provide the most solid . . . evidence, to conclude that HPV is not only the central cause of cervical cancer worldwide but also a necessary cause,"[6] states Nubia Muñoz, the study's primary author.

It is important to note that HPV does not always cause cancer. In fact, it usually does not. But it appears to be a necessary precondition. Once the virus is present, other risk factors may combine to push a woman toward cervical cancer.

Human Papillomaviruses (HPV)

Like all viruses, human papillomaviruses are tiny infectious agents. They are too small to see with any but the most powerful microscopes. Papillomaviruses are not considered to be life forms because they cannot grow or reproduce on their own. They can, however, infect host cells and "hijack" their reproductive facilities. Due to details of their shape and chemistry, HPVs usually choose cells of the human skin and mucus membranes for this job. The infected cells become little virus factories, pumping out a steady stream of new viruses that can start fresh infections in nearby areas.

The HPV family contains more than 150 different virus types. The types are referred to by number (1, 2, 3, and so on). All types of HPV are transmitted by skin-to-skin contact between an infected person and an uninfected person. They infect men and women equally. Most types go unnoticed, causing no signs or symptoms in the areas they affect. Some types cause warts or other unsightly growths on the hands and feet or in the genital area.

This electron micrograph shows a human papillomavirus. HPVs do not cause cancer but appear to be a necessary precondition for the development of cervical cancer.

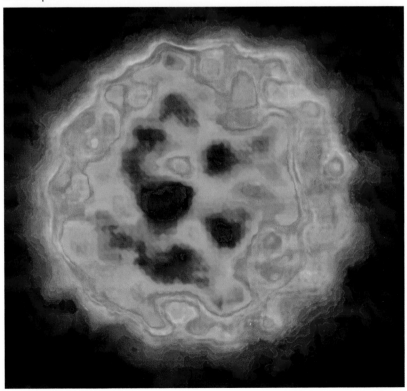

A Clear Link

The HPV/cancer link was discovered by a German virologist named Harald zur Hausen. In 1976 zur Hausen published a paper speculating that this link existed. He proved it in 1983–1984, when he isolated first HPV-16 and then HPV-18 from cervical cancer tumors. By doing so, zur Hausen identified the viruses responsible for at least 70 percent of all cervical cancer cases.

At first other virologists did not believe zur Hausen's findings. But the evidence mounted as the years went by, and even the greatest skeptics were forced to admit that zur Hausen was right. The German's research received the ultimate seal of approval in 2008, when zur Hausen received the Nobel Prize in Physiology or Medicine for his groundbreaking discovery.

German virologist Harald zur Hausen accepts the 2008 Nobel Peace Prize in Medicine for his work in identifying the viruses responsible for 70 percent of all cervical cancer cases.

As a group, HPVs are common in the human population. Researchers estimate that 70 to 80 percent of all people will host some form of HPV by the time they reach the age of fifty. "It's the common cold of the [sexually transmitted infection] world," explains scientist Ann Burchell. "If you leave the house in the winter you're probably going to catch a cold at one point. And HPV is very much like that. If you're sexually active, you're quite likely to get it at one point in your life."[7]

Many people who contract HPV do not know they are infected. Perhaps they carry a symptom-free type of HPV, or perhaps they carry a worse strain that is lying dormant (in other words, it is present, but not causing an active infection). Other people do have symptoms, but fail to realize that these symptoms are caused by HPV. "I thought my [genital] warts were calloused skin and did not pay attention to them,"[8] remembers one woman who was later diagnosed with HPV.

For any of these reasons, HPV carriers may not be aware of their condition. As a result, they take no steps to avoid passing the virus to other people. This is true of both genital HPVs and strains that affect other areas. Handshake by handshake, kiss by kiss, and sexual encounter by encounter, the infection spreads to the carrier's partners, friends, family, and even casual acquaintances.

The HPV/Cancer Link

Most HPV infections are harmless. They do no permanent damage, and they often go away on their own. Warts and other blemishes can be embarrassing, especially if they occur in the genital area, but they are not dangerous to the carrier.

A few types of HPV, however, are more worrisome. Fifteen different strains are known to cause infections that sometimes lead to cervical cancer. The worst strain is type 16, which causes about half of all cervical cancer cases. Type 18 causes another 15 to 20 percent of all cases. The remaining 30 percent of cervical cancer victims carry HPV types 31, 33, 35, 45, 58, or a handful of other strains. Collectively, these strains are known as high-risk. They are also said to be oncogenic, which is a medical term meaning they can cause cancer.

High-risk HPVs do not just cause cervical cancer. In women they can also lead to cancer of the vulva and vagina. In men they can cause penile cancer. In both sexes they may lead to cancers of the mouth, throat, and anus. They can also cause a dangerous condition called recurrent respiratory papillomatosis, in which wartlike growths infest the respiratory system. As a group these noncervical disorders strike more than 28,000 people in the United States alone each year.

All of these conditions are serious and even potentially deadly. Thankfully, they are also worst-case scenarios. Very few HPV infections develop into major disorders. Among women, just one out of every five hundred HPV carriers (or roughly 0.2%) will develop cervical cancer. Still, it is important for HPV carriers to keep a close eye on their condition. "Learning about the impact of HPV really helped me to understand why I developed cervical cancer,"[9] says a woman named Misty, who is convinced that her HPV diagnosis helped doctors catch and treat her cervical cancer early.

HPV Infection

Like all HPV strains, high-risk HPVs spread via skin-to-skin contact. These viruses infect only human mucosal (mucus-producing) cells. Mucosal cells are found inside the genital tract, the respiratory system, the anus, and other areas that are not open to casual contact. Only during sexual activity do these cells usually touch another person's skin. High-risk HPVs, therefore, are spread almost exclusively by sexual intercourse and other types of intimate contact, such as oral or anal sex. In other words, they are considered to be sexually transmitted infections.

Most cervical HPV infections are spread by male/female vaginal intercourse (although a woman can also spread the virus to another woman). During this activity viruses from the infected partner's genitals contact the skin of the uninfected partner's vagina and cervix. The viruses cannot attach themselves to the skin's tough upper layers. Sometimes, though, they find tiny breaks or tears in the skin. They may enter these gaps and make their way to the softer cells of the skin's basal

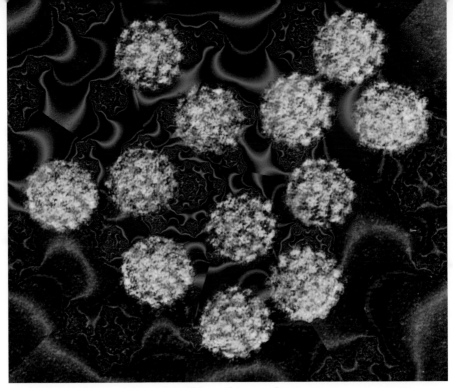

HPVs are shown in green and blue. Skin-to-skin contact can transmit HPV infection from one person to another.

layer. They can easily latch onto these cells and start the replication process.

If viruses reach the cervix's transformation zone, the job is even easier. The cells in this area are already soft and vulnerable. A high-risk HPV can easily settle in and launch an infection.

Once an HPV infection has been established, it hangs around for a long, long time. No one is sure exactly how long. Some experts believe that the body's immune system can wipe out HPV infections over the course of months or years. Others believe that HPV infections never truly disappear; they simply become inactive. The viral particles are still lurking in the host's cells, ready to leap into a new host when the opportunity arrives.

In terms of damage, the period of active HPV infection seems to be the most important factor. HPVs harm their host cells in subtle ways when they replicate. If an infection persists for a long time, the affected cells may start to look and act abnormal. These changes herald the early stages of mild cervical dysplasia, which may eventually progress into cervical cancer.

The Role of Safer Sex

While HPV infection is the number one risk factor for cervical cancer, a woman's sexual habits are a close second. This is true because risky sexual behaviors increase the chances that a woman will contract HPV, which in turn makes it possible for the woman to develop cervical cancer one day.

Scientists have identified many links between sexual behavior and cervical cancer. They know, for example, that women who have many sexual partners are more likely to develop cancer. Women who choose high-risk partners (those who, because of their past or current actions, are likely to be HPV-positive) are also at increased risk. The same is true of women who become sexually active during their teen years. This is the case partly because women who start having sex at a young age tend to have more sexual partners over their lifetimes. Also, as discussed in Chapter One, a teen's cervix is not fully developed. It is especially vulnerable to HPV infections that may become cancerous as the years go by.

Failure to use condoms is another behavior that makes it easier to catch HPV. Condom use is, therefore, an essential part of sexual safety. It is important to note, however, that condoms do not always work. Even if a couple takes every possible precaution, HPV can—and often does—find a way to spread.

This was the case for a young woman who was diagnosed with HPV during her first gynecological appointment. "I don't understand how I could have HPV!?" she exclaims on an Internet message board. "I only had sex three times altogether, and all times a condom was used. . . . I just don't understand."[10]

Risky Choices

A woman who contracts a high-risk HPV has laid the groundwork for cervical cancer. Still, by understanding the risk factors, HPV-positive women can avoid bad choices and reduce their chances of developing a more serious condition.

Smoking is one important risk factor for cervical cancer. Studies have shown that smoking harms the immune system, making it harder for a woman's body to fight an HPV infection. Also, smoking releases a chemical called nicotine into the bloodstream. Nicotine sometimes breaks down into cancer-causing chemicals that can be stored in a smoker's cervical mucus. Together with the underlying HPV infection, these chemicals can irritate and damage the cells of the cervix, leading to cancerous changes. It is estimated that smokers are three to four times more likely than nonsmokers to develop cervical dysplasia. They are twice as likely to develop cervical cancer.

Long-term use of oral contraceptives has also been linked to cervical cancer. Studies show that women who take birth-control

Studies have shown that smoking harms the immune system, making resistance to HPV more difficult.

pills for five to ten years are four times more likely to develop cervical cancer than are short-term users. This finding is a bit controversial. Many long-term contraceptive users became sexually active at a young age, and they tend to have multiple sex partners. Because both of these behaviors are risk factors for HPV, it is impossible to directly link birth-control use to cervical cancer. The relationship is strong enough, though, to be taken into consideration. Most doctors recommend annual checkups for women who use oral contraceptives, just in case.

The same is true for women who have had five or more children. Mothers in this group seem to be more susceptible to cervical cancer than women with fewer children. Although the reasons are not clear, researchers suspect that hormonal changes during pregnancy may suppress the immune system. This would make it easier for HPV infections to get out of control or for precancerous cells to change into dangerous malignancies.

Poor nutrition and/or obesity have also been linked to cervical cancer. People who do not consume enough fruits, vegetables, and essential vitamins are at greater risk than those who eat healthy diets. Obese people are more cancer-prone as well, and they are more likely to die if they do fall victim to this disorder. In a 2003 study of nearly sixty thousand cancer patients, researchers found that the death rate from cervical cancer (as well as other types of cancer) rose along with a woman's weight-to-height ratio or body mass index (BMI).

Luckily for HPV-positive women, none of these risk factors are set in stone. It is possible to lose weight and eat better. It is possible to stop smoking, switch birth-control methods, or choose to have fewer children. These choices are not always easy. But with determination, many healthy changes can be made. This was the case for Alisa, who was diagnosed with HPV at age nineteen. After her diagnosis, Alisa says, "I vowed to treat my body with respect. . . . I began taking vitamins every day, got more sleep, quit drinking and smoking, and ate good foods. I read books on how to strengthen my immune system and learned everything there is to know about [HPV]. . . . Your body can heal itself in miraculous ways, but only if you give it the right tools to do so."[11]

Unavoidable Risks

Women may be able to control some cervical cancer risk factors. Not every factor, unfortunately, is under an individual's control. Some women face unavoidable conditions or circumstances that increase their chances of developing cervical cancer.

Low socioeconomic status is unquestionably the most important of these conditions. Some women live in poor countries or regions where health care is not readily available. Others simply cannot afford health care. These women may skip their annual gynecological checkups in order to put food on the table, or to buy clothing for their children, or to pay for other basic necessities. Many of these women know they should be taking better care of themselves. As author Jennifer Chait points out, however, "It's all good and well to preach about the benefits of gynecological exams, but if you can't afford one, you can't."[12] Women in this situation can progress symptom-free from mild dysplasia to advanced cancer before they get worried enough to seek medical help.

Conditions that weaken the immune system also contribute to the development of cervical cancer. Infection with HIV, the virus that causes AIDS, is the most common cause of this problem. Organ-transplant patients and other people who take immune-suppressing drugs are also at risk. Immune-deficient people are more likely to contract HPV infections or to experience runaway cancer development.

A few women have an increased risk of cervical cancer due to certain drugs taken by their mothers. From 1941 to 1971, doctors sometimes prescribed a medicine called diethylstilbestrol (DES) to pregnant women. It was thought that DES reduced the risk of miscarriage. Studies later showed that DES did not prevent miscarriages. The same studies also showed that the daughters of women who had taken DES were more likely to develop cervical adenocarcinomas. Research is now underway to find out if the granddaughters of DES users are similarly affected.

Advancing age, the final risk factor for cervical cancer, is something no one can control. Statistics show that a woman's risk of developing cervical cancer rises sharply after age twenty-five. It continues to rise until age forty, after which it levels off. The risk then remains constant until it drops again in the senior years.

Age itself is probably not the important part of this equation. The key factor is the age at which a woman acquires a high-risk HPV, which is closely linked to the age at which she becomes sexually active. According to the U.S. Centers for Disease Control (CDC), nearly half of all high school seniors have had sexual intercourse. By age twenty-four, that figure has risen to 90 percent. It takes more than ten years for most HPV infections to develop into cancer. Nine out of ten women, therefore, should expect to hit their peak risk of cervical cancer somewhere between age twenty-five and their late thirties —which is exactly what the statistics show.

This hysterosalpingogram shows the typical T-shaped uterus malformation caused by DES. Daughters of women who took DES are more likely to develop cervical adenocarcinoma.

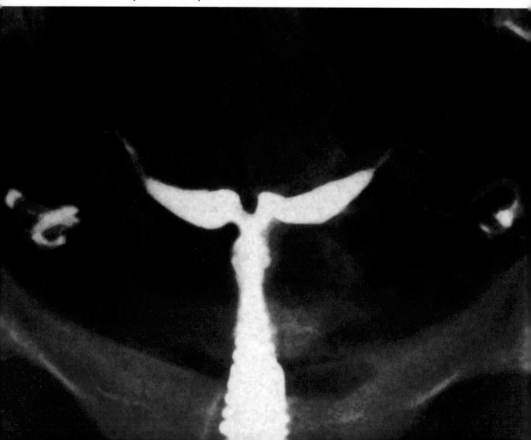

Carrying a Killer

Cervical cancer is a women's disorder. However, men play an important role in the spread of this disease. They are just as likely as women to carry HPV. If an infected man has many sex partners, he can put countless women at risk of developing cervical cancer.

Researchers have discovered some interesting links between men and cervical cancer. They have found, for example, that a man's current partner is more likely to develop cancer if one of the man's previous partners was affected. They have also learned that circumcised men are less likely to carry HPV. One 2009 study found that the risk was up to one-third lower in this group.

This finding sheds light on another statistic. Scientists have known for a long time that cervical cancer occurs less frequently among Jewish women. It now appears that ritual circumcision is the reason. Nearly all Jewish men are circumcised as infants, so it makes sense that HPV—and, by extension, cervical cancer—would be less common in this group.

What Are the Chances?

Risk factors can help to predict a woman's chance of developing cervical cancer. But a prediction—even a strong one—is not a sure thing. In the United States only about twelve thousand women were diagnosed with cervical cancer in 2005 (the most recent year for which figures are available). This means that millions upon millions did not develop the disorder, even though many of them undoubtedly lived risky lifestyles.

Statistically speaking, then, cervical cancer may not be the biggest problem facing women today. But it is still an important one. Caught late, cervical cancer can be deadly. Caught in the dysplasia stage, it is virtually always curable. For this reason, every woman should know the facts about cervical cancer and take charge of her reproductive health.

CHAPTER THREE

Detecting and Diagnosing Cervical Cancer

In the early 1900s cervical cancer struck an estimated 30 to 40 out of every 100,000 women each year. The disorder was not usually detected until symptoms appeared. By this point, an affected woman might be seriously ill. Even with prompt treatment, cervical cancer patients often died from their disorder.

The outlook is much better for today's women. Doctors now have tools that can detect cervical abnormalities before they become cancerous. As a result, problems can be treated and eliminated before they get too serious. Through early detection and diagnosis, the incidence of cervical cancer in developed countries has dropped nearly 75 percent since the mid-1940s. Today, only 8 out of every 100,000 American women will be diagnosed with cervical cancer each year.

The Pap Test

Today, the most important tool in the fight against cervical cancer is the Pap test. This test is sometimes also called the Pap smear. It is named after George Papanicolaou, the Greek doctor who perfected the procedure in the 1930s and early 1940s. Introduced to the medical community in 1943, the Pap test was immediately adopted by doctors everywhere. It quickly became the favorite diagnostic tool for cervical cancer and has held that position to the present day.

A Pap test is done as part of a routine gynecological exam. To prepare for the test, a patient lies on her back on an examination table with her knees bent. She places her heels in special footrests. The doctor then inserts an instrument called a speculum into the woman's vagina. The speculum separates the vaginal walls so the doctor can see the woman's cervix. After a quick visual exam, the doctor inserts a small spatula or brush into the cervix's external os and twirls the tool to scrape off some tissue. From start to finish, this process takes just seconds, and it is usually painless for the patient.

Once the doctor has obtained a tissue sample, he or she may swab it onto a glass slide. The doctor may also rinse the swab

A doctor holds Pap test instruments. The speculum, left, and the cytobrush, right, allow the doctor to take samples of cells from the cervix.

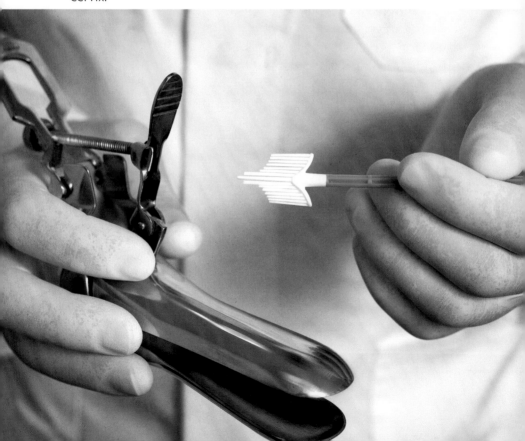

in a liquid-filled vial. The sample is then sent to a laboratory, where it is prepared for viewing.

When the preparation is complete, a specialist called a cytopathologist examines the sample under a microscope. He or she determines whether the cervical cells are normal or whether they show signs of abnormality. If abnormal cells are found, the cytopathologist notes the degree of abnormality—whether it is mild, severe, or somewhere in between. He or she also determines what percentage of the sample is abnormal.

As the final step, the cytopathologist prepares a report that summarizes his or her findings. The report uses a scale called the Bethesda System, which was introduced in 1988 to standardize Pap results. Bethesda System categories range from "Normal" (no unusual changes noted) to "Invasive carcinoma." Abnormalities that are probably caused by an infection or irritation are categorized as "Reactive changes." Changes that occur for no clear reason are dubbed "ASCUS" and "AGUS," which stand for "Atypical squamous cells of unknown significance" and "Atypical glandular cells of unknown significance." Dysplasias from mild to severe are described as "SIL," which stands for "Squamous intraepithelial lesion." SILs are further divided into "LSIL" (low-grade dysplasias) and "HSIL" (high-grade dysplasias).

Every now and then a Pap slide is difficult to read. When this is the case, the cytopathologist rates the test as "Unsatisfactory." This rating does not mean that the actual cells are unsatisfactory. It simply means that the results are inconclusive. In these cases, a doctor may ask the patient to return to the office for another Pap test. The doctor may also choose to wait a few months before retesting, depending on the patient's risk factors and health history.

The HPV DNA Test

When a doctor is worried about a patient's Pap result, he or she may order an HPV DNA test as a follow-up. Called the Hybrid Capture II or hc2 test, this procedure can be done using the same sample provided for the Pap test. It identifies genetic material from most high-risk HPV strains. If a patient tests neg-

Pap Results and Their Meanings in the Bethesda System

- **ASCUS (atypical squamous cells of unknown significance).** Some squamous cells from the outer layer of the cervix look abnormal. The cause is unknown but could include irritation or infection with HPV or another agent.
- **ASC-H (atypical squamous cells, may include high-grade lesions).** Some squamous cells from the outer layer of the cervix look abnormal. The cause is unknown but could include high-grade lesions.
- **LSIL or LGSIL (low-grade squamous epithelial lesion).** Squamous cells are minimally abnormal but are not likely to become cancerous.
- **HSIL or HGSIL (high-grade squamous epithelial lesion).** Squamous cells are moderately to severaly abnormal and are likely to become cancerous if not treated. This diagnostic category includes CIS (carcinoma in situ).
- **AGC (atypical glandular cells).** Some glandular cells from higher up in the cervical lining look abnormal. This is a more serious finding than ASCUS.
- **AIS (adenocarcinoma in situ).** A precancerous lesion exists in the glandular tissue of the cervix.

Adapted from D. Solomon, et al., "The 2001 Bethesda System: Terminology for Reporting Results of Cervical Cytology," *Journal of the American Medical Association*, vol. 287, No. 16, April 24, 2002, pp. 2114–19.

ative for these strains, she almost certainly does not have cancer or a precancerous condition. If she tests positive, cervical cancer is a possibility. Based on these findings, the patient's doctor can decide what further steps to take.

HPV testing is a recent development. In the United States this procedure was approved in March 2003. Since that time it

A technician analyzes samples from a Pap test. HPV DNA testing has been highly successful in detecting cervical cancer.

has become increasingly popular among medical professionals, and it is not hard to see why. The HPV test is easy and inexpensive. It is also reliable, with an accuracy rate approaching 95 percent. When Pap and HPV tests are done together, the chance of detecting cervical abnormalities is nearly 100 percent. Patients who receive dual screening are, therefore, better off than those who get only the Pap test.

Dual screening had lifesaving consequences for a woman named Micheline. During a routine checkup, Micheline received both a Pap test and an HPV test. Her Pap results came back negative, but the HPV test was positive. Micheline's doctor recommended doing a recheck in six months, just to be safe. The recheck revealed that Micheline was still positive for HPV—and now her Pap test showed abnormal cells as well. This result worried the doctor. Even though Micheline's cervix looked healthy, he decided to do more extensive testing. To his surprise, the tests showed that Micheline had cervical adeno-carcinoma.

Micheline's condition could have become deadly. Because it was caught early, however, treatment was straightforward and effective. Micheline credits the HPV test for this result. "I thank God every day that I tested positive for HPV," she says. "Because of that test, my doctor was so persistent. . . . If I hadn't had the HPV test, I know things would have turned out differently. The cancer would have likely had a chance to persist longer unchecked, and I might not have been cured so easily."[13]

Micheline may seem extraordinarily lucky. But actually, her experience is not unusual. In the few short years since the HPV test was introduced, women and doctors everywhere have become convinced of its value. Alan Welt, Micheline's physician, counts himself among that number. "It is one thing to read stories about the benefits of HPV testing, and another to have the HPV test prove to be a life-saving test for one of your own patients. Micheline's story reinforces my belief in the benefits of routine HPV screening,"[14] he says.

Most major medical organizations are convinced as well. They are releasing guidelines for the use of the HPV test in standard health care. In the United States, for example, the Food and Drug Administration (FDA) currently recommends routine HPV testing for women aged thirty and older. Women under thirty do not need consistent screening. For this group, the test is recommended as a follow-up to a worrisome Pap result.

Taking a Closer Look

When a doctor is concerned about a patient's Pap or HPV DNA results, he or she may schedule a procedure called a colposcopy. During this procedure, the doctor takes a close-up look at the patient's cervix. He or she searches for the telltale signs of cervical cancer.

Causes of Abnormal Pap Results

HPV infection is the most common cause of abnormal Pap results. It is not, however, the only cause. Pap test results can also be judged abnormal due to any or all of the following conditions:

- **yeast infection:** This condition is caused by a fungus called *Candida albicans*. Symptoms include vaginal itching and discharge.
- **bacterial infection:** Bacteria from the rectum sometimes find their way into a woman's reproductive system. Infection and abnormal Pap results may follow.
- **trichomonas infection:** Caused by the sexually transmitted protozoan *Trichomonas vaginalis*, this condition is characterized by vaginal irritation.
- **intrauterine device (IUD) usage:** IUDs are small birth-control devices inserted into the uterus through the cervix. IUDs can sometimes irritate the cervix and cause false-positive Pap results.
- **advancing age:** After menopause, natural cervical cell changes called atrophic vaginitis occur. Pap tests can detect these changes and report them as unidentified abnormalities.

A colposcopy is performed in the doctor's office. To prepare for this procedure, a patient lies on the exam table just as she does for a Pap test. The doctor inserts a speculum and separates the walls of the vagina. He or she then looks at the cervix through a tool called a colposcope, which is like a lighted pair of binoculars. First, the doctor uses low magnification to get a sense of the cervix's shape and overall health. Next, the doctor switches to higher magnification to see details of the cervical surface and particularly the transformation zone, where the majority of cervical cancers begin.

It can be hard to spot cervical abnormalities. To make the job easier, doctors often wash the cervix in an acid solution. The acid is weak—about like vinegar—and it does not hurt the patient. It does, however, make areas of dysplasia turn white. Doctors may also swab the cervix with an iodine solution. This solution stains normal skin, but it does not affect abnormal tissue. Using these changes as a guide, the doctor has a better idea of where to look for signs of trouble.

Sometimes no signs of trouble appear. In these cases, the colposcopy is said to be negative. At other times, though, a doctor spots abnormal blood vessels, lesions, or growths. When this happens, the doctor takes samples from the abnormal area or areas. One way to collect samples is by doing a punch biopsy, which involves snipping off one or more small skin pellets. Another way is to perform an endocervical curettage (ECC), during which skin cells are scraped off the surface of the endocervical canal. The pellets or cells are preserved and sent to a laboratory for further analysis.

A colposcopy is not a major procedure. It takes just ten to fifteen minutes and is not usually painful. Some women do report cramping or pinching feelings if biopsies are done, but others feel nothing at all. "At one point I asked [my doctor] to tell me when the painful part was coming. She said she had already done that part and I was almost done,"[15] writes one woman on an Internet message board.

Still, the idea of a colposcopy and possible biopsy is very frightening to some patients. "I was terrified. Not of what might be found, but of the procedure! . . . Only after the gynecologist promised she'd use a local anesthetic and would stop the procedure if it was too traumatic did I agree to have it done,"[16] remembers a woman named Jax.

It was not easy for Jax to overcome her fear. Once the procedure was over, however, she admitted that her worries had been groundless. "The biopsy was painless. My trust level with this physician went up,"[17] she reports. Most important of all, the test results came back normal, freeing Jax from the specter of possible cervical cancer.

Success by Repetition

Although the Pap test has revolutionized the detection and diagnosis of cervical cancer, it is far from a perfect tool. Experts estimate that between 20 and 50 percent of all Pap tests return false negatives. This means that the results are reported as normal even though precancerous or cancerous cells are actually present. False negatives are mostly due to human error. If a sample contains just a small percentage of abnormal cells, a busy lab worker can easily miss the early signs of trouble.

Luckily for women everywhere, the Pap's high failure rate is not a serious problem. It usually takes years for cervical cancer to develop. During this period a woman who gets regular gynecological checkups will have many Pap tests. The chances of every test failing are tiny, especially if a woman's cervical abnormalities are worsening and becoming easier to notice. With repetition, Pap testing is nearly 100 percent effective in detecting precancerous changes.

Loop Electrosurgical Excision Procedure (LEEP)

Not all women are as lucky as Jax. Some patients will be diagnosed with cervical intraepithelial neoplasia (CIN) following a biopsy procedure. If the condition is mild (CIN I), the doctor will probably take a wait-and-see approach. If it is moderate or severe (CIN II or CIN III), the doctor will probably recommend further treatment to stop the condition from worsening.

The most common treatment for moderate dysplasia is the loop electrosurgical excision procedure, which is called LEEP for short. This procedure is usually done in the doctor's office. To perform LEEP, the doctor inserts a wire loop through a speculum to the patient's cervix. An electrical current is passed through the loop. The wire quickly becomes very hot—so hot, in fact, that it can burn cleanly through flesh. The doctor uses the superheated wire as a knife, simultaneously shaving off suspicious tissue and cauterizing (searing closed) the wound that remains.

LEEP is more invasive than a simple biopsy. For this reason, many women fear that it will be more painful as well. Most patients, though, feel very little sensation during the procedure. "This was not nearly as bad as I thought it would be. I experienced no pain to speak of,"[18] wrote a woman on an Internet message board. Many women do experience cramping, similar to menstrual cramps, and light bleeding after LEEP. These occurrences are normal and pass within a day or two.

Once a LEEP procedure is finished, the doctor puts the removed tissue into a liquid preservative. The sample is sent to a lab, where a pathologist examines it under a microscope. The pathologist looks carefully at any abnormal cells to see if they appear cancerous. He or she makes a note of anything unusual. Later, the pathologist's notes will be included in a report that summarizes the situation.

The pathologist's report will also include important information about the sample's edges, or margins. A sample with no abnormal cells near the edges is said to have negative or clean margins. Clean margins usually mean that the doctor removed all of the dysplasia. A sample that shows abnormalities right up to its edges is said to have positive margins. Positive margins usually mean that some dysplasia remains in the cervix. When this is the case, further treatment may be needed to solve the patient's problem.

Cryotherapy

A procedure called cryotherapy is sometimes used as a follow-up to LEEP. It may also be performed instead of or at the same time as LEEP. In cryotherapy, the doctor uses liquid nitrogen to supercool a metal instrument. He or she then presses the instrument against abnormal cervical tissue and holds it there for several minutes to chill the cells underneath. This process is repeated until all visible abnormalities are frozen solid.

The frozen cells thaw out when the cryotherapy treatment is complete. They do not, however, return to their normal function. Too damaged to survive, the cells start to flake away from the cervix. They trickle out of the vagina in a watery discharge that may continue for several weeks. If the treatment is successful, all of the patient's dysplasia will be gone when this process is complete.

Like LEEP, cryotherapy is not usually uncomfortable. Some women do experience moderate menstrual-like cramps during the procedure. These cramps are a reaction to the freezing process. They typically go away when the cryotherapy treatment ends.

In cryotherapy, a liquid nitrogen-cooled metal instrument is held against abnormal tissue, freezing it and destroying the cancerous cells.

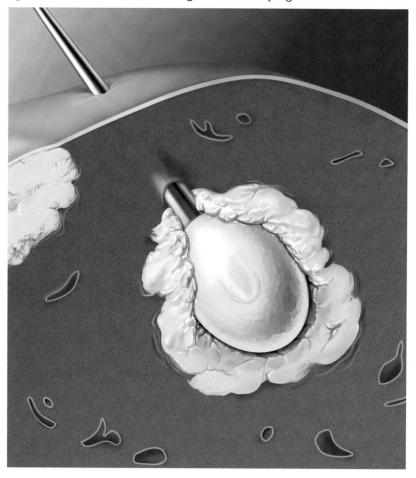

Conization

Sometimes a patient's dysplasia is too severe to be treated with LEEP or cryotherapy. When this is the case, the woman's doctor may choose to perform a cone biopsy or conization instead.

Conization is done in a hospital with the patient under general anesthetic. During the procedure a surgeon uses a laser or a scalpel to remove the tissue surrounding the lower part of the endocervical canal. He or she then uses sutures to seal the surgical wound. The procedure gets its name from the shape of the cutaway tissue, which looks something like an upside-down ice cream cone. This cone is sent to a laboratory, where a pathologist examines its margins and cell makeup for abnormalities.

Conization is a much more extensive procedure than LEEP or cryotherapy. It is not surprising, therefore, that patients who undergo this procedure have more postsurgical issues. Moderate to heavy vaginal bleeding is common and usually lasts for about a week. Spotting or discharge may continue for another one to two weeks. Some pelvic pain is possible as well. To minimize these symptoms, patients should not do anything strenuous for at least a week after the procedure. They should also avoid tampons, sexual intercourse, or anything else that might irritate the surgical site for at least three weeks. By following these simple steps, women should recover from conization without any major trouble.

Problem Solved?

LEEP, cryotherapy, and conization all have the same purpose. Used properly, they can eliminate moderate to severe cervical dysplasias—often forever. "I had the LEEP procedure about 15 years ago. . . . It saved my life. I was on my way to full-blown cervical cancer. Since the procedure, I have not had one bad Pap,"[19] reports a woman on one Internet message board.

Freedom from dangerous dysplasias is unquestionably a good thing. It is not, however, without cost. All dysplasia treatments can leave scars on the cervix, making future Pap tests harder to interpret. LEEP and conization can also shave the cervix dangerously thin, especially if they are done more than once. "I've had young patients come to me with hardly any cervix left because they've had so many LEEP procedures. . . . Too many doctors take too much extra tissue when they do LEEP,"[20] complains gynecologist Ira Horowitz of Emory University's Winship Cancer Institute in Atlanta, Georgia. A thinner cervix is more likely to fail during pregnancy, so women who receive LEEP or conization miscarry more often than women who have never undergone these procedures.

Many women would be happy to take this risk in exchange for a cancer-free life. This result, however, cannot be guaranteed. In some cases cervical abnormalities return a year or two after treatment. In others, lab results show that the abnormalities were never fully removed. Either way, further treatment is needed to stop the dysplasia from progressing.

Sometimes the lab results are even worse. They show that a patient's condition has moved beyond dysplasia to invasive cancer. When this is the case, a woman must brace herself for a new battle. Together with her doctor she will embark on a quest to track and treat her cervical cancer.

CHAPTER FOUR

Tracking and Treating Cervical Cancer

When abnormalities break into the deep tissues of the cervix, they are no longer considered dysplasias. They are reclassified as invasive carcinomas. Informally, they are known simply as cervical cancers.

It can be terrifying to receive a diagnosis of cervical cancer. A woman named Susan vividly remembers the moment she heard the news. "I was shocked when my doctor first told me I had cancer. I couldn't believe it was happening to me. It was the worst moment of my life,"[21] she says.

Like Susan, many cervical cancer victims feel shock, fear, and dread when they learn about their condition. These feelings are perfectly understandable. Cervical cancer does, after all, kill nearly half of its victims. It is important to understand, however, that the term *cervical cancer* does not mean the same thing for every patient. Some women are in the earliest stages of cancer when they are diagnosed. They have many treatment options and a very high probability of success. Other women are in later stages, which means fewer effective treatments are available. These women face a more difficult struggle and a lower chance of long-term survival.

All cervical cancer victims, even those whose condition is advanced, have a few things in common. They do have options, they can be treated, and they have the possibility of being cured. By promptly tracking and treating malignancies, any woman can increase her chances of beating cervical cancer.

Tracking Cervical Cancer

When a woman is first diagnosed with cervical cancer, she knows very little about her overall situation. LEEP and conization simply show that cancer is present and identify its type. They do not provide any information about whether the cancer has spread beyond the cervix, and if so, how extensively. A doctor must know these things before he or she can determine the right course of treatment for a patient. Before tackling her cervical cancer, therefore, a woman undergoes one or more procedures to shed more light on her condition.

A thorough pelvic examination is the simplest test a doctor might choose. This procedure is much more extensive and more painful than a regular pelvic exam, so it is usually done under general anesthetic. During the test the doctor takes

In a thorough pelvic examination the doctor closely examines (clockwise) the vagina, cervix, and uterine cavity and palpates the patient's abdomen.

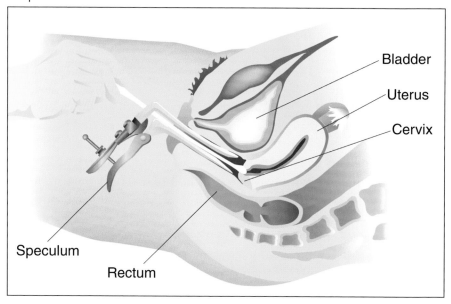

close-up looks at the patient's vagina, cervix, and sometimes her uterine cavity. He or she also palpates the patient's abdomen. If anything irregular is found, either by sight or by feel, the doctor notes it for further investigation.

Sometimes a doctor suspects that cancer may have spread into the patient's intestinal tract. When this is the case, a procedure called proctoscopy may be performed. In this procedure, a lighted tube that acts like a flexible microscope is inserted into the patient's anus. The doctor peers into the tube's viewing end to see details of the anus, rectum, and lower colon. Biopsies are taken if the doctor spots any worrisome growths.

A similar test called cytoscopy can detect cancer that has spread into the urinary tract. This test uses the same techniques and tools as proctoscopy but examines the patient's urethra and bladder instead of the intestinal tract. Through visual examination and biopsy, if necessary, the doctor determines if cancer is present.

Urography is another test that may be performed on the urinary tract. In this procedure the patient is injected with a special chemical that shows up clearly on X-rays. The kidneys absorb the chemical and send it through the urinary system. By taking X-rays throughout this process, technicians can obtain precise pictures of the patient's kidneys, bladder, and the associated tubes. A radiologist examines the pictures for signs of cervical cancer.

X-ray and other imaging techniques are useful for more than just urography. Doctors can use them to get a big-picture view of a patient's body as well. X-rays of a patient's lungs, skeleton, and lymph nodes, for instance, can show whether cervical cancer has spread to these areas. Computerized tomography, or CT scans (also called CAT scans), use X-rays along with computers to produce digital images of a patient's lymph nodes. Magnetic resonance imaging, or MRI scans, use magnetic energy and radio waves to create cross-sections of certain organs or body parts. Finally, positron emission tomography, or PET scans, use radioactive chemicals to capture three-dimensional images of a patient's body processes. By combining some or all of these tools, a doctor can build a very complete picture of a patient's condition.

Stages of Cervical Cancer

Once a doctor understands the extent of a woman's cancer, he or she can identify its stage. This word has a specific meaning in cancer terminology. It describes the precise severity of a cancer based on its location, size, routes of spread, and other factors. Different criteria apply to different types of cancers and are established by different organizations. In the case of cervical cancer, staging guidelines are set by the International Federation of Gynecology and Obstetrics (FIGO). Used world-wide, FIGO guidelines ensure that cervical cancer patients everywhere are evaluated on an equal basis.

The FIGO staging system is very simple. It sorts cervical cancers into categories from Stage 0 (precancer or carcinoma in situ) to Stage IV (invasive carcinoma that has spread beyond the pelvic wall). Stages I, II, III, and IV are further broken down into subcategories that describe small differences between one phase of development and another. In Stage IA, for example, the carcinoma is too small to see with the naked eye. In Stage IB, the tumor is in the same general area, but it has grown enough to be spotted during a visual exam.

The staging process can be very helpful to cervical cancer patients. It slots a frightening and often confusing condition into tightly defined categories. By doing so, it gives women a way to understand what is happening to their bodies. "I felt better after reading more detailed information. . . . I located good medical and scientific [Internet] sites and was reassured to read that the rate of cure for [my stage of] cervical cancer is fairly high,"[22] says a woman named Margaret.

Staging is not only useful for the patient, of course. It is an essential piece of knowledge for the doctor as well. A woman's options are very different depending on the stage of her cancer. For this reason, proper staging is a critical part of a patient's diagnosis and, subsequently, her treatment process.

Treatment for Microinvasive Cancers

The earliest phase of cervical cancer is described as Stage IA1. This stage is also sometimes called microinvasion. It is characterized by very small, shallow growths. Women in Stage IA1

FIGO Stages of Cervical Cancer

Stage	Substage
I The cancer is confined to the cervix.	**A1** The cancerous area is less than 3mm deep and 7mm wide. **A2** The cancerous area is between 3mm and 5mm deep and less than 7mm wide. **B1** The cancerous area is visible but is not larger than 4cm. **B2** The cancerous area is visible and is larger than 4cm.
II The cancer extends beyond the cervix but is still contained within the pelvic area.	**A** The cancerous area includes the upper part of the vagina but not the lower third. **B** The cancer has spread to the tissue next to the cervix (the parametrial tissue).
III The cancer extends onto the pelvic wall or into the lower third of the vagina.	**A** The cancerous area includes the lower third of the vagina but not the pelvic wall. **B** The cancerous area includes the pelvic wall.
IV The cancer extends beyond the pelvis.	**A** The cancerous area includes the bladder or rectum. **B** The cancer is recurrent or has spread to distant organs.

International Federation of Gynecology and Obstetrics, "Staging Classifications and Clinical Practice Guidelines for Gynaecological Cancers," October 10, 2006, p. 55. www.figo.org/files/figo-corp/docs/staging_booklet.pdf.

have many treatment options. If the cancer appears in just one tiny spot, it can usually be removed by LEEP or cone biopsy, which double as treatments for small lesions. In some cases the cancerous cells can also be frozen off with cryotherapy. After these procedures the patient receives regular checkups to make sure the cancer has not returned.

Some Stage IA1 malignancies show signs of spreading to a woman's lymph nodes or vaginal wall. When this is the case, treatment will be more aggressive. It will usually involve a surgery called hysterectomy, which is the removal of the patient's cervix and uterus. By taking out these organs, the surgeon hopes to eliminate every scrap of cancerous material.

Types of hysterectomy.

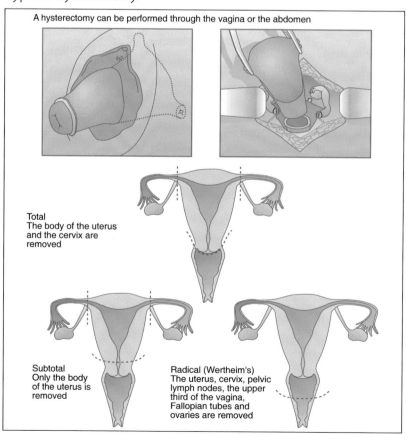

A hysterectomy can be performed through the vagina or the abdomen

Total
The body of the uterus
and the cervix are
removed

Subtotal
Only the body
of the uterus is
removed

Radical (Wertheim's)
The uterus, cervix, pelvic
lymph nodes, the upper
third of the vagina,
Fallopian tubes and
ovaries are removed

The second phase of cervical cancer is called IA2. Like Stage IA1, Stage IA2 is considered a microinvasion. Lesions in this stage are no wider than those in Stage IA1, but they extend a bit deeper into the cervical tissues. This means the risk is greater that they have spread in ways the doctor cannot see. When a patient's cancer reaches this stage, therefore, more drastic steps are usually recommended. The standard treatment for women in this group is radical hysterectomy, which includes the removal of some lymph nodes, ligaments, and the upper part of the vagina along with the cervix and uterus.

Hysterectomy and radical hysterectomy are major procedures. Women can expect to stay in the hospital for two or three days when having these surgeries. Full recovery takes up to six weeks. On an Internet message board, one hysterectomy patient told another woman what to expect: "For the first two weeks there is quite a bit of pain. . . . After about three weeks you'll feel a lot better. By four weeks you'll probably not feel any more pain. By six weeks I can tell you that you feel like you did before the operation."[23]

Recovery time is not the only issue women face when considering hysterectomy. They must also consider the fact that by removing the uterus, they are giving up their ability to become pregnant. Older women or those who do not want children may not see this as a problem. For younger women, though, hysterectomy can be devastating. "[It was] the most heartbreaking decision of my life. I don't think I will ever get over this,"[24] says one hysterectomy patient.

Cervical cancer patients who feel this way sometimes choose a procedure called radical trachelectomy instead of hysterectomy. In this surgery, the cervix and the upper part of the vagina are removed. The uterus is then reattached to the vagina. Most trachelectomy patients are able to get pregnant. Because the cervix is missing, however, these women often cannot carry their babies to term. A 2007 study found that about one-third of all post-trachelectomy pregnancies end in miscarriage.

Some women are not willing to take this chance. For these women, hysterectomy without removal of the ovaries may be an option. This procedure lets a woman keep her eggs, which can be harvested and fertilized later. The fetus is then carried to term by a surrogate mother. Preserving the ovaries also prevents the patient from going into early menopause, which occurs when ovarian hormones disappear.

Treatment for Moderately Advanced Cancers

If cervical cancer is not caught in the microinvasive stage, it will develop into a more serious condition. Cancers from Stage IB to IIA are considered to be moderately advanced. They are characterized by larger lesions and a greater likelihood of spreading beyond the cervix. Doctors will treat these cancers aggressively to stop them from spreading any farther. Radical hysterectomy plus pelvic lymphadenectomy (removal of the pelvic lymph nodes) is the standard surgery for moderately advanced cervical cancer.

Depending on the precise stage of the cancer, radiation therapy may also be necessary. This treatment exposes cancerous cells to radioactive waves. The radiation damages the cells' DNA, with the result that the cells soon die. With luck, all of the cancerous tissue will be destroyed with minimal damage to healthy areas nearby.

Two different types of radiation therapy can be used with cervical cancer patients. The most common type is external radiation. During this procedure a machine shoots a radioactive beam at the patient's pelvis. The beam is carefully positioned to ensure that it radiates the cancerous area. This procedure is done on an outpatient basis. It takes fifteen to twenty minutes and is generally repeated several times per week for up to six weeks.

Some cervical cancer victims undergo a procedure called internal radiation. For this procedure, a woman must be admitted to the hospital. A capsule of radioactive material is placed directly in the woman's cervix. The capsule remains in place for several days, thoroughly irradiating the surrounding tissues and, ideally, destroying all cancerous matter. The capsule is removed before the patient is released.

Complementary Therapies

Surgery, radiation, and chemotherapy are the only officially approved treatments for cervical cancer. Many women, however, have reservations about these methods. They feel that a natural approach is better. These women often choose complementary therapies to support or even to replace traditional treatment.

A carefully balanced diet is one popular choice. For cervical cancer patients, some experts recommend a diet high in beta carotene, selenium, vitamin C, and other nutrients. Fresh vegetables and fruits, whole foods, and certain teas and herbs are also thought to be helpful. Proper eating can boost the body's immune system while mitigating the unpleasant side effects of conventional treatments.

Acupuncture may have a similar effect. In this therapy an acupuncturist uses slender needles to stimulate different parts of the patient's body. Many patients report increased energy and decreased discomfort following this procedure.

Not all complementary therapies deal with the patient's physical health. Some are designed to help women cope with the

mental aspects of cancer treatment. Counseling, hypnotherapy, biofeedback, and/or spiritual support can make patients feel better. By doing so they give these patients much-needed strength to continue their fight against cervical cancer.

Acupuncture may help the body's immune system, increase energy levels, and decrease discomfort.

Radiation therapy is very effective for reducing or eliminating local tumors. When the cancer has spread beyond a small area, however, radiation alone may not be sufficient. For patients in late Stage IB or Stage IIA, a treatment called chemotherapy is often recommended in addition to surgery and radiation. In this procedure, cancer-killing chemicals are injected into the patient through an intravenous tube. Because the chemicals travel through the bloodstream, they reach and affect every part of the patient's body. They have the potential to destroy cancerous cells wherever they may be hiding.

Like radiation therapy, chemotherapy takes place over time. It is done in bursts, with alternating treatment and recovery periods. The specific chemicals, dosage, and number of treatment/recovery cycles vary from one patient to another.

Treatment for Advanced Cancers

When cervical cancer has clearly spread into the tissues surrounding the cervix, it is upgraded once again. It is now a Stage IIB cancer. This stage, and those that follow it, are considered to be advanced. They demand immediate and very aggressive treatment if the patient is to have any hope of survival.

Treatment for advanced cancer does not usually include surgery. It is too late for this approach to do much good. Instead, doctors will order a combination of external and internal radiation along with chemotherapy. The treatments are given together over a six- to seven-week period. This combined approach gives patients the best possible chance of wiping out their cancer and of long-term survival.

The road to this result is often rocky for patients. Radiation and chemotherapy have many unpleasant side effects that can make treatment nearly intolerable for some women. Pelvic radiation, for instance, often causes fatigue, nausea, and lost appetite. It can even burn the patient's flesh. "By the end of the fifth week [of treatment], my inner thighs and pelvic area were so burned that I had open, oozing blisters,"[25] recalls a woman named Rena.

Chemotherapy, too, is often difficult. Common side effects

The side effects of chemotherapy include nausea, vomiting, hair loss, and exhaustion.

of this treatment include hair loss, nausea, vomiting, and extreme exhaustion. A cervical cancer patient named Marcy remembers these feelings all too well. "At one point, I couldn't walk to the end of my driveway and back without stopping to rest. At times when I took a shower, just the weight of the water hitting me on the head felt almost unbearable. Smells were another thing that drove me crazy. I had this horrible, gritty taste in my mouth, and I felt like I had the worst case of morning sickness possible,"[26] she says.

These symptoms might seem like a reasonable tradeoff if radiation and chemotherapy were guaranteed cures. But unfortunately for Marcy and others in her situation, this is not the

Support Groups

Even with the support of friends and family, women often feel alone in their fight against cervical cancer. Sometimes they were reluctant to share their frustration and stress with loved ones. At other times they feel that no one in their immediate circle truly empathizes with their situation. "Those who haven't been through something similar just don't understand," says a cancer survivor named Karen.

To combat this situation, many women turn to support groups. In these groups, cervical cancer victims come together in person or online to share their feelings and experiences. They talk, laugh, and cry. In doing so they form emotional bonds that may be missing in other areas of their lives.

Karen remembers how she felt when she found an online gynecological cancer support group. "It was amazing to me that there were other women out there who had been through similar things, and who shared similar fears. Being in contact with others, and learning more about [gynecological] cancers and their treatments has really helped me in dealing with those fears," she says.

Karen, "My Story," Eyes on the Prize, May 2000. www.eyesontheprize.org/stories/karen.html.

case. Sometimes cancerous lesions shrink during treatment but fail to vanish altogether. In other cases a patient's cancer does disappear, only to reappear a few months or years later.

Cancer that fails to respond to treatment is called Stage IVB or recurrent cancer. Whether it can be re-treated depends on details of the recurrence. If the area of cancerous tissue is very small, radiation and chemotherapy are sometimes helpful. If the recurrence is widespread, though, these therapies are not likely to do much good. Many women with end-stage cervical cancer, therefore, reject further treatment. They choose a palliative (pain-reducing) approach instead. By dulling the worst of the pain, morphine and other drugs let untreatable patients spend their final months in relative comfort. In the end, they can also allow these patients to pass away quietly, with peace and dignity.

Cervical Cancer Prognosis

Cervical cancer can be deadly. Worldwide, about 55 percent of cervical cancer patients die as a result of their condition. This does not mean, however, that every woman has a 55 percent chance of death. The prognosis varies depending on the stage at which the cancer is detected.

Cancer mortality statistics are described as five-year survival rates. These numbers refer to the percentage of cancer victims who, if treated, will still be alive in five years. For Stage I cervical cancers the five-year survival rate is between 80 and 90 percent. For Stage II cancers the rate is between 60 and 75 percent, and for Stage III cancers it ranges from 30 to 40 percent. The outlook becomes very grim indeed for patients who have Stage IV cancer. Somewhere between 0 and 15 percent of these women will be alive five years after their initial diagnosis.

Five-year survival rates can be terrifying to patients. It is important to remember, however, that these numbers are just statistics. They do not carry an automatic death sentence. Just ask Leslie. Five years after learning about her Stage IV cancer, Leslie shared her story of survival on a cancer-support Web site. "I am disease free. . . . So far I have beaten the odds, and so can you. Remember that someone has to be in the 2 or 5 or 20 percent who survive, and it might as well be you,"[27] she says.

Leslie is right. Cervical cancer may be a potential killer, but even the worst cases are not hopeless. With a positive attitude and proper treatment, any woman has the potential to conquer cervical cancer.

CHAPTER FIVE

Preventing Cervical Cancer

Once cervical cancer takes hold, it can be very difficult to cure. Hundreds of thousands of women lose their lives to this disorder each year. These women's deaths, says the World Health Organization (WHO), are "a sad and unnecessary loss to their family and their community. Unnecessary, because there is compelling evidence that cervical cancer is one of the most preventable forms of cancer."[28]

Doctors may have the knowledge and tools to prevent cervical cancer, but they cannot do the job on their own. They need patients to be proactive about their health care—to know their risk factors, to seek regular screening, and to take advantage of new tests and vaccines. By doing these simple things, every woman can reduce or even eliminate her risk of developing cervical cancer.

Regular Screening

Getting regular gynecological checkups is the single most important thing a woman can do to prevent cervical cancer. Most gynecologists and health insurance companies recommend yearly exams for every woman, regardless of her age or medical history. These exams are not intended to detect cervical cancer alone. They also screen patients for other reproductive

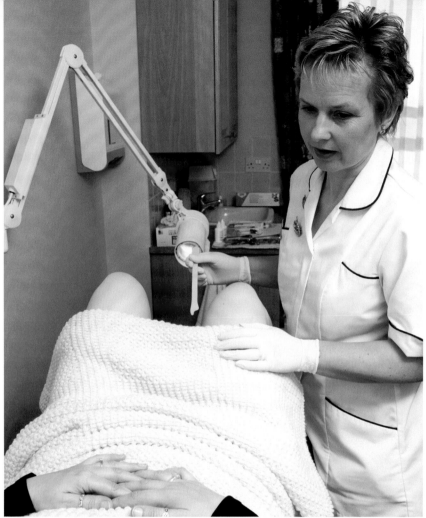

A gynecological nurse performs a Pap test on a patient. All women, especially young women, should get regular pelvic screening.

cancers along with yeast infections, skin irritations, and many other conditions.

Not all women need cervical cancer screening at every checkup. The frequency of Pap tests and other procedures depends on a number of factors. According to guidelines released by the American Cancer Society (ACS), young women require the most frequent testing. The ACS guidelines state that all women should begin cervical cancer screening about three years after they begin having vaginal intercourse, but no later than when they are twenty-one years old. Screening should be done every year with the regular Pap test or every two years using the liquid-based Pap test, which is a more sensitive diagnostic tool.

The guidelines change when a women reaches age thirty. After this age it is safe for women who have had three normal Pap results in a row to reduce their screening. They may choose to get tested every two to three years instead of annually. Another reasonable option for women in this category is to get screened every three years with either the conventional or liquid-based Pap test, plus the HPV DNA test. Women who have certain risk factors such as DES exposure before birth, HIV infection, or a weakened immune system should continue to be screened annually.

The guidelines change once again for women age seventy or older. Women in this group who have had three or more normal Pap tests in a row and no abnormal Pap test results in the last ten years may choose to stop screening for cervical cancer. As with younger women, an exception is made for patients with a history of cervical cancer, DES exposure before birth, HIV infection, or a weakened immune system. These women should continue to be screened as long as they are in good health.

The final category under the ACS guidelines involves women who have undergone hysterectomies. Women who have had a total hysterectomy (which includes removal of both the uterus and cervix) can stop having cervical cancer screening, unless the surgery was done as a treatment for cervical cancer or pre-cancer. Women who have had a partial hysterectomy (during which the uterus is removed, but the stump of the cervix remains) should continue to be screened according to their age categories.

The ACS guidelines are simple and straightforward. They can dramatically reduce a woman's risk of cervical cancer—if they are followed. It is all too easy, however, for busy women to postpone or ignore their gynecological appointments. "I didn't get regular Pap tests. I knew that I was supposed to, but I just had too much going on in my life,"[29] remembers one woman who developed cervical cancer after years of skipping her exams.

This type of attitude is frustrating to medical professionals. Obstetrician and gynecologist Craig L. Bissinger speaks for many of his colleagues when he says, "It's hard to believe that there are still millions of women who fail to keep up with annual check-ups. Prevention of disease, with an annual Pap smear, is the most effective medicine possible against cervical cancer."[30]

After age thirty, women should have a Pap test every three years.

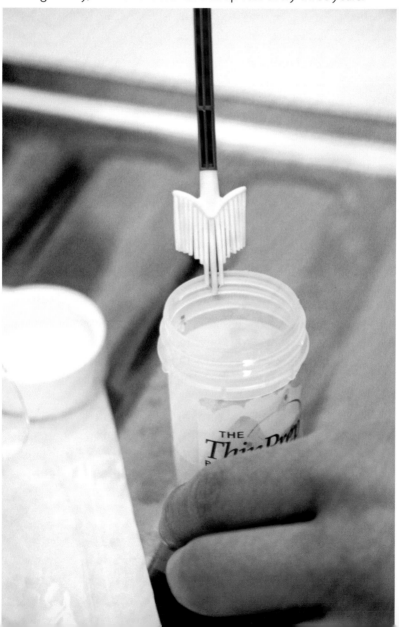

Expanded HPV Testing

It would be hard to find a doctor who did not support proper screening for cervical cancer. Exactly what constitutes proper screening, however, is currently the subject of much debate. Today, many doctors have come to believe that the Pap test is overused and inefficient. They feel that combination Pap/HPV testing or even HPV testing alone are better choices. Cosette Wheeler, a University of New Mexico School of Medicine professor who has made a career out of studying HPV, holds this view. "The time has come that we need to make a conversion [to the HPV test]. It would be doing women a disservice not to,"[31] she says.

This perspective is supported by a scientific study published in April 2009. In this study, researchers administered a single HPV DNA test to tens of thousands of women in India. The women received treatment based on their individual results. After eight years, the experimental group was found to have about half the normal rate of advanced cervical cancer and death. Meanwhile, women who received annual Pap tests also had reduced cancer rates but were still much more likely to develop cancer than women in the HPV-testing group.

This finding has far-reaching implications. If just one HPV test is a better predictor of cervical cancer than repeated Pap tests, women could safely reduce their number of gynecological checkups. "You could start screening women at [age] 30 and do it once every 10 years,"[32] says Rengaswamy Sankaranarayanan, the study's chief author. This would be especially helpful in poor nations, where many women cannot afford annual care.

Recognizing this fact, medical organizations everywhere are endorsing Sankaranarayanan's work. One typical statement of support appeared on the editorial page of *The New England Journal of Medicine*. "The implications of the findings of this trial are immediate and global: International experts in cervical-cancer prevention should now adapt HPV testing for widespread implementation. Low-resource countries do not need to establish large [Pap] programs whose effectiveness requires repeated screening,"[33] wrote Mark Schiffman and Sholom Wacholder of the (U.S.) National Cancer Institute.

The same is true in developed countries, where standard gynecological practices could change quickly if doctors embrace solo HPV testing. Many medical professionals do not merely think that this should be the case, as Wheeler suggests. They believe that it will be—and soon. The demonstrated success of HPV testing, says Paul D. Blumenthal of Stanford Medical School, is "another nail in the coffin" for Pap smears, which will "soon be of mainly historical interest."[34]

Other medical professionals do not think the end is quite so near. They point out that many gynecologists are reluctant even to cut back on Pap tests according to the ACS guidelines, much less eliminate them completely. "We haven't been able to get doctors to go along [with reduced Pap testing]," says Debbie Saslow, director of gynecologic cancer for the American Cancer Society. "When you've been telling everyone for 40 years to get an annual Pap smear, it's hard to change."[35]

Change, however, is probably inevitable. As it comes, one thing seems certain: The effects of increased HPV DNA testing will be positive. This procedure pinpoints the patients at greatest risk for cervical cancer, thus allowing doctors to provide appropriate and early care. By asking for or agreeing to HPV testing, women everywhere can take strong steps to protect themselves from cervical cancer.

Vaccination Against HPV

Despite its proven benefits, HPV testing is limited in one important way. It does not actually do anything to prevent cervical cancer. It merely identifies women who are in danger. Women who test positive for high-risk HPVs can be carefully monitored, but nothing can change the fact that they carry a potentially cancer-causing infection.

Recent developments in the fight against cervical cancer are likely to change this picture. Since 2006, vaccines against the most dangerous and widespread HPV strains have been available in many countries. Given by injection, these vaccines mimic the shape and behavior of the HPV virus. The

Clinical Trials for Cervical Cancer

Researchers are constantly developing new treatments for all types of cancer, including cervical cancer. These treatments are tested through programs called clinical trials. Cancer patients sometimes enroll in these trials, hoping that experimental drugs or procedures will be more effective than known regimens.

A clinical trial has four possible phases. Phase I usually includes a small number of healthy volunteers. It is designed to test the effects of the product on humans, including how it is absorbed and excreted. This phase also tests for side effects.

Phase II involves up to several hundred patients. In this phase one group of patients receives standard treatment; another group receives the experimental treatment. After a period of several months or years, researchers compare the groups' results to find any differences.

Phase III is similar to Phase II but more extensive. Phase III trials often involve several thousand patients. Large-scale testing provides more accurate results and more information about possible side effects. When Phase III testing is complete, a pharmaceutical company can ask the U.S. Food and Drug Administration (FDA) to approve the product for public sale.

After a product reaches the general market, it may undergo Phase IV testing. During this phase a company compares the new product to treatments already on the market, monitors its long-term effectiveness, and determines whether it is cost effective. The company may change its marketing plan based on these findings or even withdraw the product if worrisome results emerge.

body fights back against the vaccine by forming antibodies that kill the invading particles. If and when real HPV appears, the antibodies—which remain in the woman's system—destroy it before infection can occur. By doing so they reduce the woman's risk of developing dysplasias and, subsequently, cervical cancer.

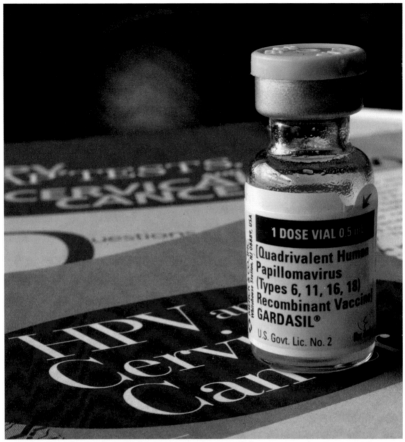

Gardasil is the only HPV vaccine approved for use in the United States and has shown to be effective in protecting women against four different strains of HPV.

In the United States, Gardasil is currently the only approved HPV vaccine. Gardasil is produced by a U.S. pharmaceutical company called Merck. It is sometimes called the quadrivalent vaccine because it protects women against four different HPV strains, including types 6, 11, 16, and 18. Types 6 and 11 cause nearly all cases of genital warts, while types 16 and 18 cause up to 70 percent of all cervical cancers. Evidence suggests that Gardasil may also provide some protection against ten additional high-risk HPV strains, although the vaccine is not specifically targeted to these viruses.

In some other parts of the world, including Australia, the Philippines, and the European Union, a vaccine called Cervarix is often used. Cervarix is produced by pharmaceutical giant GlaxoSmithKline, which is based in the United Kingdom. The vaccine is sometimes called bivalent because it is designed to protect women against just two high-risk HPV strains, 16 and 18. Like Gardasil, however, Cervarix seems to work against some other oncogenic strains as well.

Gardasil and Cervarix are very effective. Both vaccines provide nearly 100 percent protection against their target viruses. Because cervical cancer vaccines are so new, no one is sure how long this effect will last. Scientists are optimistic, however, that vaccinated women will prove over time to have long-lasting immunity. If this is the case, the impact of vaccination could be very great indeed. As the (U.S.) National Cancer Society (NCS) puts it, "Widespread vaccination has the potential to reduce cervical cancer deaths around the world by as much as two-thirds, if all women were to take the vaccine and if protection turns out to be long-term."[36]

Most women, of course, do not take such a broad view. They focus more on what the vaccine might mean in their own lives. Shannon, who chose to be vaccinated after weeks of research, describes her feelings in an online video interview. "After it was done I had this huge sense of relief and was so glad that I had done it, because I really felt empowered. I was hopefully bettering my health for the future,"[37] she says.

The immense popularity of Gardasil and Cervarix suggests that many women agree with Shannon. By early 2009 an estimated 44 million doses of Gardasil had been produced and sold. Total Cervarix sales were lower but still in the millions. These numbers show that women everywhere are eager to enjoy the protection offered by cervical cancer vaccines.

Permanent Protection?

This protection, unfortunately, has limits. The most important limitation is that vaccination blocks only the two most dangerous HPV strains. It has some effect against other strains—but only some. This means that a woman who has received Gardasil or Cervarix injections is still vulnerable to at least thirteen high-risk HPVs. Together these strains cause 30 percent of all cervical cancer cases. Vaccination, therefore, reduces a woman's chance of cancer by about 70 percent but does not eliminate it. To put it plainly: A vaccinated woman can still get HPV, and she can still develop cervical cancer.

The very nature of cervical cancer vaccines is another roadblock to their use. Gardasil and Cervarix are prophylactic vaccines, which means they prevent viruses from getting a foothold in the body. To accomplish this job the vaccines must be given before a woman encounters the targeted HPVs. Medical professionals strongly recommend, therefore, that women seek vaccination before they become sexually active. Since HPVs are so common, virgins are the only patients who are guaranteed to receive full protection from HPV vaccination.

In the United States, FDA regulations underscore this fact. Gardasil is currently approved only for girls and women between the ages of nine and twenty-six. After this period so many women have been exposed to HPV that vaccination is no longer practical as a general rule. Older women can still benefit if they know for sure that they are HPV-free. Under the current guidelines, however, insurance will not pay to vaccinate these patients.

This was the case for a woman named Meg, who was too old to qualify for Gardasil. "I decided to have the vaccine after testing negative for HPV. Because I'm outside the target age range, insurance didn't cover the vaccine. However, I have a couple of good friends who were diagnosed with cervical cancer. If possible, I'd like to avoid going through the same experiences,"[38] she writes on an Internet discussion board.

Women who share Meg's feelings may soon have more options. As of mid-2009 the FDA was considering a request to extend Gardasil's approved age range. Merck officials believe that Gardasil is safe and effective for women up to age forty-five. If the final data from clinical trials support this belief, it is likely that the FDA will approve the change. This would mean that more women could seek vaccination—and be reimbursed for it—if they felt it was the right choice in their particular circumstances.

Vaccinate the Boys, Too

Routine HPV vaccination for girls is a good first step toward conquering cervical cancer. Many medical professionals believe, however, that the vaccine should be offered to boys and young men as well. They point out that by carrying HPV from one sex partner to another, men play a very important role in the spread of cervical cancer. This role could be greatly reduced if men were immune to the highest-risk HPV strains.

Male vaccination would not just reduce cervical cancer rates. It would have direct benefits for men, too. If Gardasil is used, one of these benefits is immunity to HPV strains 6 and 11, which cause 90 percent of all genital warts. Most men would be glad to avoid this condition, which can be unsightly and embarrassing.

HPV vaccination would also give men some protection against certain cancers. It would reduce the risk of penile and oral cancers, and would eliminate up to 90 percent of all anal cancers. This effect would be most marked in the gay population, where sexual behaviors promote the spread of HPV in the anal area.

Keeping Yourself Safe

Health organizations do not take much notice of individual choices. They make recommendations that they feel will do the most good for the most people. In the United States the current American Academy of Pediatrics guidelines call for routine vaccination of all eleven- and twelve-year-old girls. Very few girls this age are sexually active, so this group is likely to get the maximum benefit from a cervical cancer vaccine.

Most pediatricians have adopted these guidelines. Whether parents and their daughters will follow them, however, is another question. Unlike many other vaccines, Gardasil is not required for school attendance. Vaccination is, therefore, a choice that each girl, with her family's help, must make for herself.

Different people have very different opinions about this choice. Some believe that vaccination is essential. "As a parent, I

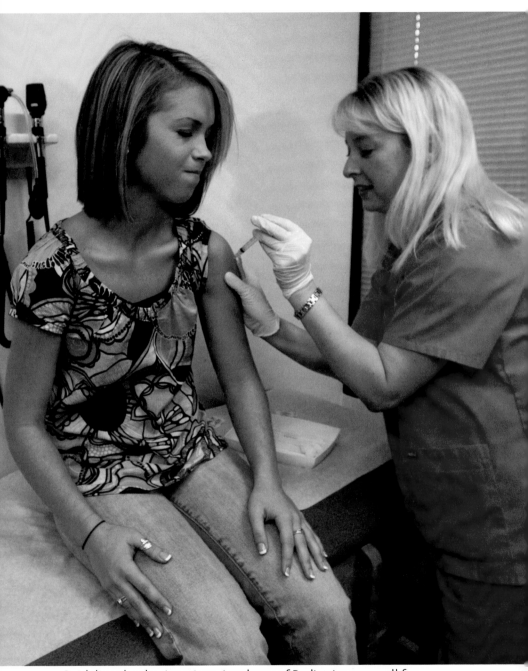

Guidelines by the American Academy of Pediatrics now call for routine vaccination against HPV of all eleven- and twelve-year-old girls.

feel it's my responsibility to do everything I can to keep my kids safe. . . . An HPV vaccine could be an important part of that,"[39] says a mother named DuWayne.

Not everyone feels the same way. Some women have concerns about vaccines in general or about cervical cancer vaccines in particular. Others wonder why they should bother with a vaccine that is not guaranteed to prevent cervical cancer. If they have to get regular screening anyway, they feel they might as well skip the shots and focus on catching dysplasias early instead.

This type of debate is natural for any new vaccine. It will probably rage for many years to come. While it does, women of every viewpoint can enjoy the fact that they have many good choices when it comes to their reproductive health. By using the prevention tools available today, women can do a great deal to protect themselves against cervical cancer.

CHAPTER SIX

Challenges to Overcome

Since the 1940s the Pap test has made it possible to detect and remove cervical abnormalities before they develop into cancer. In recent years vaccination and HPV testing have made it even easier to stop cervical cancer in its tracks. As a group these tools create many exciting possibilities in the field of cervical cancer prevention and treatment. Internist Stephen J. McPhee of the University of California, San Francisco, speaks for many health professionals when he says, "Cervical cancer shouldn't be a cause of death anymore, in fact it shouldn't be a problem anymore."[40]

It is undeniable, however, that cervical cancer still is a problem. This is the case mostly for practical reasons. Prevention and treatment programs can be hard to implement because they are too costly or too controversial. Even when they are implemented, they may be underused, misunderstood, or even rejected outright. All of these challenges must be overcome before the world can be free of cervical cancer.

A Third-World Scourge

Cervical cancer takes the highest toll in underdeveloped nations, where many people cannot afford consistent health care or do not understand its importance. Southeastern Africa and

A Bolivian woman waits at a clinic for a medical consultation on cervical cancer. Woman in Bolivia are many times more likely to get cervical cancer than women in the United States.

northwestern South America are the world's hardest hit regions. In these places up to 68 out of every 100,000 women will be diagnosed with cervical cancer each year. Central America, many Caribbean nations, Melanesia, and much of Asia (most notably India and Bangladesh) are also danger spots. Women in these areas are up to ten times more likely to develop cervical cancer than those who live in the United States and other developed nations.

Lack of screening is the biggest reason for this difference. A woman who lives on the African plains or high in the mountains of Peru may not have easy access to modern medical care. Even if she does have access, she may view checkups as troublesome and unnecessary. As writer and doctor Shobha S. Krishnan points out, "A traditional Pap smear screening can be . . . cumbersome, requiring three visits when an abnormal result occurs: one for the Pap smear, a second for a colposcopy follow-up and biopsy, and the third for treatment."[41] Women who are busy tending farms or raising large families are all too likely to skip this process unless bothersome symptoms make it absolutely necessary.

Money may also be an issue for women in poor areas. Without health insurance, many of these women simply cannot afford Pap testing and other cervical cancer screens or treatments. This was the case for Pratibha, an Indian woman who received screening only after a free clinic was established in her town. "If any expense was involved, I would never have thought of participating or discussing it with my husband,"[42] she says.

In some places cultural norms can also present roadblocks to cervical cancer screening. Women may be too embarrassed to expose their private parts to a doctor. They may feel that cancer is shameful or a punishment for past misdeeds. They may also worry that they will become the subject of gossip if they seek treatment. According to a cancer survivor named Ava, this is very much an issue on the island nation of Trinidad and Tobago, where patient confidentiality is not guaranteed. "This is a small country, and [cervical cancer] is a very private problem that you would want to keep private. . . . This would add more pressure to what is already a distressing and embarrassing situation,"[43] she says.

Overcoming the problems of medical availability, cost, and perception can be a daunting task. Still, many nations are currently tackling this challenge. Widespread education and Pap programs have been launched in Mexico, Chile, Thailand, Singapore, and some parts of sub-Saharan Africa. The results of these programs have been mixed, with some areas seeing improvement and others seeing little change. It is hoped that results will improve over time as patients and doctors alike become more educated about cervical cancer prevention.

Demographic Differences

Better education is important not only in poor nations. It is also needed in developed countries, where certain groups of women continue to have a much higher incidence of cervical cancer than others.

In the United States ethnicity and race are strongly related to cervical cancer. The United States Cancer Statistics (USCS) division of the CDC reports that Hispanic and Latino Americans are most susceptible to this disorder. Between 2001 and 2005 (the most recent period for which figures are available) an average of 13.2 per 100,000 Hispanic women developed cervical cancer each year. This group was closely followed by African Americans, with a rate of 11.6 per 100,000 cervical cancer victims annually. Other studies suggest that American women of Vietnamese, Korean, and native Alaskan heritage are also at increased risk compared to white women, who averaged 8 cases of cervical cancer annually per 100,000 women.

Geography, too, is related to a woman's cervical cancer risk. USCS statistics show that cervical cancer is more common in the Middle Atlantic states of New Jersey, New York, and Pennsylvania, for instance, than it is in the Northeast. It is even more prevalent in the Southeast and the Southwest. A few regional hot spots also stand out as high-risk areas. Women from rural Appalachia (which encompasses eastern Kentucky, northern Tennessee, and West Virginia) and those living along the Texas/Mexico border, for example, were found to have a much higher-than-usual incidence of cervical cancer.

Ethnic and geographic differences are not actually caused by a person's race or location. They are the result of behaviors, attitudes, and conditions that are more common among these groups. One study showed that African Americans, for instance, are less likely as a group than white women to return for follow-up procedures after an abnormal Pap test. This behavior puts some African American women at an increased risk for cervical cancer.

In rural Appalachia, where most residents are white, the problem is tied to money and lifestyle choices. Many women from this area live in extreme poverty, without access to regular medical care. They are also more likely than other groups to smoke cigarettes and less likely to get enough exercise. Combined, these risk factors have a noticeable effect on Appalachian cancer statistics. An average of 10.7 per 100,000

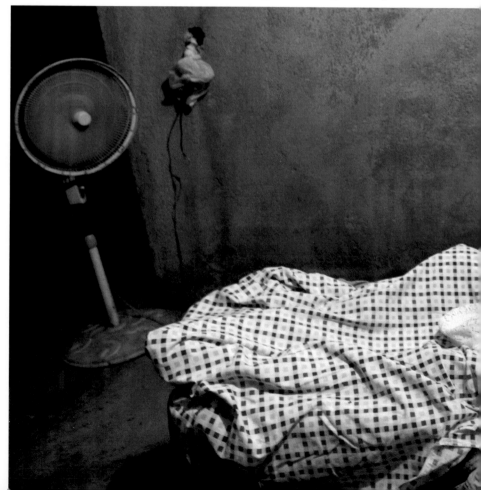

women from this group are diagnosed with cervical cancer each year.

As in underdeveloped countries, education will play an important role in solving these problems. The education effort, however, must be targeted to the women who need it most. "Public officials will have to include more effective strategies in reducing the racial, ethnic, and regional disparities. . . . Awareness programs such as culturally sensitive cancer education, prevention, and screening measures should be instituted in addition to addressing the global burden of the disease,"[44] says Krishnan.

A young Mexican woman with cervical cancer is comforted by her mother. Hispanic women as a group are nearly twice as susceptible to cervical cancer as white women.

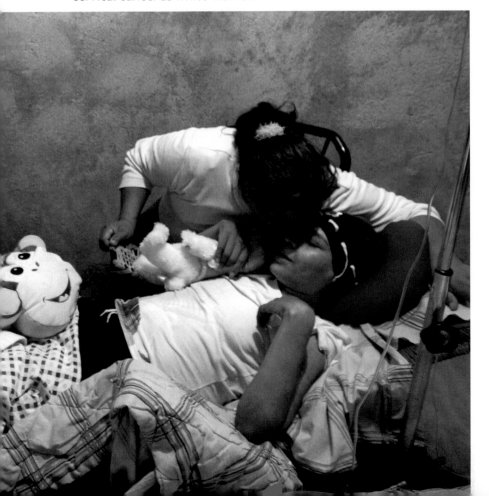

A Vaccine for All?

It might seem that the "global burden," as Krishnan puts it, could be reduced tremendously through widespread HPV vaccination. Statistics suggest that cervical cancer rates would drop to less than one-third of their present levels if all women received the vaccine. This result looks good on paper. In real life, however, it will be hard to achieve. Many barriers must be overcome before HPV vaccines will be available to every woman.

Of these barriers, cost and opportunity are the most significant. The issues are just the same as they are for cervical cancer screening. Women who do not have easy access to medical care may have trouble completing the HPV vaccination series, which includes three shots spread over a six-month period. They also may not be able to afford the shots, which currently cost $120 (U.S. dollars) each. In many nations the three-shot sum of $360 is more than a year's salary for an average worker. It is unrealistic to expect women in this position to seek vaccination unless it is part of a subsidized program.

In wealthier countries the financial burden does not loom quite so large. Health insurance or socialized health care programs cover the cost of vaccination for many women in these areas. Completing the three-shot HPV series, however, is still an obstacle. In early 2009 a study of England's vaccination program showed that about 12 percent of the girls who received the first shot skipped the second. Figures were not available for the third shot, but the skipped percentage is undoubtedly higher in this group. Without completing the series, girls are not fully protected from the vaccine-targeted HPVs.

Concern About Side Effects

Practical problems are not the only barriers to widespread HPV vaccination. The public's perception, too, is a major issue. In particular, many women worry that Gardasil and Cervarix may do more harm than good. "I have a 15-year-old daughter, and I will NOT be getting her this vaccine. I don't think it's been out long enough for people to know what the side effects will be later in life," says a mother on one Internet

Case Study: The Hepatitis B Vaccine

The current debates over Gardasil and Cervarix are all too familiar to medical professionals. They are almost identical to discussions that took place decades ago, when a vaccine against a virus called hepatitis B (HBV) was introduced.

HBV, which causes chronic liver infection and sometimes cancer, is spread mostly through sexual contact. It can also be transmitted by the sharing of contaminated needles, which often occurs during illegal drug use. For these reasons, HBV vaccination created a great deal of controversy when it was approved in 1982. Parents felt the vaccine was inappropriate for their children, as many parents feel about HPV vaccination today.

Over the years, however, it became clear that the health benefits of HBV vaccination greatly outweighed the risks. By the early 1990s the World Health Organization (WHO) and many other associations, including the CDC, were recommending immunization for all newborns. As the new guidelines were implemented and the public got used to the drug, the debate died down. Today, most parents do not hesitate to protect their children from HBV. Vaccination advocates hope that the same will be true someday of HPV.

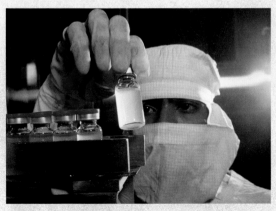

A technician checks the quality of mass-produced hepatitis B vaccine. Some people object to giving the vaccine to pre-adolescent children.

U.S. Human Services secretary Alex Azar announced the approval of Gardasil vaccine for use in June 2006. This announcement kicked off a firestorm of public debate that continues to the present day.

message board. "More research needs to be done, and even though the FDA OK'd it, I don't trust something this new."[45]

Other parents have gone along with vaccination, only to be dismayed by the apparent negative results. "This vaccine made my daughter very ill—fainting, vomiting, fever after just one shot. Needless to say, she will not be getting any follow ups,"[46] said one mother after her daughter received a Gardasil injection.

Accounts like these along with a number of well-publicized incidents have added fuel to the anti-vaccination fire. Critics of HPV vaccines point especially to the cases of Jenny Tetlock and Whitney Baird, teens who died of suspiciously similar neurological problems after receiving Gardasil. Jenny and Whitney are two of more than twenty American girls who died soon after receiving the drug.

In late 2008 the FDA and CDC reviewed these cases as a group. They did not find a common pattern to the deaths. They did find underlying health problems, including diabetes, heart failure, drug use, and more, in nearly all of the cases. This evidence suggests that the girls who received the drug would have died anyway, with or without HPV vaccination. Researchers concluded, therefore, that Gardasil was not the cause of death.

The FDA and CDC have also studied reports of less serious side effects after Gardasil usage. Reported effects include fainting, pain and swelling at the injection site, headache, nausea, and fever. These effects probably are related to the vaccination, at least some of the time. The FDA and CDC emphasize, however, that they are no more serious or common than the side effects associated with other well-accepted vaccines. "While there is no such thing as a completely safe medical product, the available evidence suggests that benefits of this vaccine outweigh the risks,"[47] says John Iskander, acting director of the CDC's immunization safety office.

Many parents refuse to accept this view. They would rather take a wait-and-see approach, giving Gardasil (and Cervarix, which is the subject of a similar debate in other countries) time to establish a longer track record. At present, however, CDC and FDA guidelines state that Gardasil is safe and effective for girls and women in the approved age range. The drug is strongly recommended for eleven- and twelve-year-old girls, who stand to benefit most from HPV vaccination.

Social Concerns About HPV Vaccination

This recommendation makes sense from a public health perspective, but it has proven to be a sticking point for many people. Some parents think it is inappropriate to vaccinate preteen girls against a sexually transmitted disease. They would be more comfortable if the guidelines recommended vaccination for older teens, who are presumably closer to the age of sexual debut. "[My daughter is] not sexually active yet. We have an agreement that she's not going to be until, hopefully, she's at least 18. I'm not saying that we won't ever get [vaccinated]. It's just that we're going to wait a bit,"[48] says Maggie, who is the mother of a fourteen-year-old girl.

Other parents do not think waiting is the right answer. They feel it is wrong to vaccinate girls against STDs at any age. They believe that strong morals and sexual abstinence provide better —and more appropriate—protection. A 2007 article from a religious organization espouses this view. "Double your efforts to help your children avoid having sex before marriage. If young people would wait to have sex until married, there would be little need for Gardasil—and certainly no need for young girls to be inoculated for an STD they should never even be exposed to,"[49] it advises its members.

Safety rather than morals is the main concern of yet another group. Some parents think that their daughters will view HPV vaccination as tacit permission to become sexually active. They also fear that their daughters might perceive the vaccine as a blanket protection against all STDs. Girls who hold this mistaken belief might be more likely to choose risky sex partners or skip condom use. By refusing HPV vaccination, parents hope to dodge these sticky issues and encourage their daughters to make better sexual decisions.

In Support of Vaccination

Supporters of the HPV vaccine disagree strongly with this viewpoint. They point out that no vaccination can protect a teen against pregnancy. Fear of this consequence alone should be enough to encourage safe sex, if girls are properly educated. Vaccine proponents also underscore the fact that even if a girl makes all the "right" choices, she can still fall victim to high-risk HPVs and, eventually, to cervical cancer. In her essay "Parental Prerogative," author Beki Benning expands on this idea:

> Good decisions fail to protect women against sexual assault, lies, and adultery every day. A virgin bride who has made good decisions all her life might still marry a man who has lied about a sexual encounter in the past. Her husband can always have unprotected sex outside of their marriage. She can always be raped walking down the street, in a parking lot, or even in her own home. As tragic and unthinkable as these scenarios might be, why would her parents choose to ignore these possibilities when the chance to protect their daughter is so readily available?[50]

Benning sums up many pro-vaccine arguments in this paragraph. Because Benning's imaginary HPV victims lead lives of impeccable morality, however, one important point is missed.

A vaccination program in Northern Ireland to immunize twelve- to thirteen-year-old girls against HPV has proved successful.

Statistics prove that most teens do engage in sexual activity at some point—and when they do, they often take great pains to hide this fact from the adults in their lives. Since parents cannot truly know their children's sexual status, vaccine supporters believe that every girl should be inoculated as a cautionary measure before she reaches sexual maturity.

The Future of Cervical Cancer

The debate over HPV vaccination is passionate and ongoing. It raises many important questions, including some that may be answered over time and others that probably will never be resolved. No matter what position a person takes on this issue,

Jade Goody (1981–2009)

Jade Goody, an outspoken fixture of British reality TV, thrust cervical cancer into the spotlight in late 2008 and early 2009. The twenty-seven-year-old Goody was diagnosed with this disorder in August 2008 while participating in an Indian version of the TV show *Big Brother*. Goody withdrew from the show to undergo more tests, which revealed that her cancer was advanced and life threatening. Over the next few months, Goody embarked upon a desperate and highly public battle to save her life. This battle, unfortunately, turned out to be a losing one. Goody died on March 22, 2009, just seven months after her original diagnosis.

Although tragic, Goody's death has had some positive results. Medical authorities in the United Kingdom report that the demand for Pap testing has skyrocketed among young women. English health ministers have also agreed to review the country's National Health Service policies on cervical cancer screening, which currently recommend testing of women ages twenty-five and older. If officials drop the age to twenty, as it stands in the rest of the United Kingdom, doctors could detect more dysplasias before they had a chance to turn cancerous.

The tragic death of Jade Goody in the United Kingdom due to cervical cancer has caused a substantial increase in Pap testing and a move toward beginning testing at the age of twenty.

however, it is undeniable that HPV vaccines expand women's options. With a few simple shots, it is possible today to dramatically reduce any woman's risk of developing cervical cancer.

The task now is to change possibility into reality. Recognizing the immense potential of HPV vaccines, organizations around the world are working to make these medications available in developing countries. They are also trying to establish Pap and HPV screening programs, which are essential even for vaccinated women. Once established, these programs could have a huge impact on the worldwide incidence of cervical cancer.

Whether this will happen depends on two things: political support and public education. Governments must be willing to fund the fight against cervical cancer before programs can even be considered, much less adopted. If and when programs do exist, women must be educated about their importance and encouraged to use them. By understanding the issues, women today have more power than ever before over cervical cancer.

Notes

Introduction: A Preventable Plague

1. Juliet V. Spencer, *Cervical Cancer*. New York: Chelsea House, 2007, p. 107.

Chapter One: What Is Cervical Cancer?

2. Shobha S. Krishnan, *The HPV Vaccine Controversy: Sex, Cancer, God, and Politics*. Westport, CT: Praeger, 2008, p. 23.
3. Millie, "Re: Cervical CIS to Vaginal Dysplasia," Cancer Compass, May 22, 2007. www.cancercompass.com/message board/message/all,9001,0.htm.
4. National Cervical Cancer Public Education Campaign, "Cervical Cancer Survivor: ' . . . Less Invasive than Getting Treated for Cervical Cancer,'" Life Stories video. www.cervical cancercampaign.org/ccfacts/videos/2.html.
5. Rena, "My Story," Eyes on the Prize, June 2000. www.eyes ontheprize.org/stories/rena.html.

Chapter Two: What Causes Cervical Cancer?

6. Nubia Muñoz, "Human Papillomavirus and Cancer: The Epidemiological Evidence," *Journal of Clinical Virology*, October 1, 2000, p. 19.
7. Quoted in Helen Branswell, "It Only Takes One: HPV Infections Common Among Women Who've Only Had One Partner," *Calgary Sun*, January 13, 2008. http://calsun.canoe.ca/News/National/2008/01/13/4770889.html.
8. Anonymous, "Lack of Information = Fear of Unknown," Genital Warts FAQ. www.genitalwartsfaq.com/personal_experiences/1637.html.
9. Quoted in University of Texas MD Anderson Cancer Center, "Just the Facts . . . HPV & Cervical Cancer," Public Edu-

cation Office, March 2008. www.mdanderson.org/patient-and-cancer-information/cancer-information/community-ser
vices/publications-and-brochures/pdfs/mda-fs-hpv-cervical-3.12.pdf.

10. Royal Girl, "I Don't Understand How I Could Have HPV!?"
Yahoo! Answers, 2008. http://answers.yahoo.com/question/
index;_ylt=AgaBwXJyjGupMeOCG4B.PgjzKIX;_ylv=3?qid=
20080209095512AAOcAN7.

11. Alisa, "I Am a Better Person Because of My STD," Sexual
Health Buzz, August 22, 2008. http://yoshi2me.com/sexual-health/ archives/i-am-a-better-person-because-of-my-std.

12. Jennifer Chait, "Women Putting Off Pregnancy Due to Bud-
get," Thrifty Mommy, May 8, 2009. www.blisstree.com/
thriftymommy/women-putting-off-pregnancy-due-to-budget.

Chapter Three: Detecting and Diagnosing Cervical Cancer

13. Micheline Fornarotto, "Micheline Fornarotto's Story," The
digene HPV Test. www.thehpvtest.com/Women-Speak-Out/digene-HPV-Test-Success-Stories/Micheline-Fornarotto
.html.

14. Alan Welt, "Dr. Welt's Perspective," The *digene* HPV Test.
www.thehpvtest.com/Women-Speak-Out/digene-HPV-Test-Success-Stories/Micheline-Fornarotto/Dr-Alan-Welt.html.

15. mseragon, "I Need a Colposcopy but Am Worried About the
Pain?" Yahoo! Answers, July 2007. http://answers.yahoo
.com/question/index;_ylt=An2Qo1CvWzryuDliaHa1TtkjzKIX
;_ylv=3?qid=20070312214536AAE2ViK.

16. Jax, "My Story," Eyes on the Prize, May 2000. www.eyesonthe
prize.org/stories/jackie.html.

17. Jax, "My Story."

18. Sugarplum, "How Painful Is a LEEP Done in the Doctor's
Office?" Yahoo! Answers, December 2008. http://answers
.yahoo.com/question/index;_ylt=AgBetFENFrg6lLkKZ_SGl.E
jzKIX;_ylv=3?qid=20081202090711AAxMJGi.

19. Caregiver, "The Leep," Cancer Compass, August 1, 2006.
www.cancercompass.com/message-board/message/all,6178,0
.htm.

20. Quoted in Jeanie Lerche Davis, "Cervix Treatment May Endanger Pregnancy Later," WebMD, May 4, 2004. http://women.webmd.com/news/20040504/cervix-treatment-may-endanger-pregnancy-later.

Chapter Four: Tracking and Treating Cervical Cancer

21. Susan, "Cervical Cancer Survivor: I Made It Through Cervical Cancer Treatment," Life Stories, video, National Cervical Cancer Public Education Campaign. www.cervicalcancercampaign.org/ccfacts/videos/9.html.
22. Margaret Tobin, "Experiences with Cervical Cancer," Oncolink, November 1, 2001. www.oncolink.upenn.edu/coping/article.cfm?c=6&s=31&ss=76&id=133.
23. Makingitup, "H*E*L*P Hysterectomy Questions!!" Yahoo! Answers, July 2006. http://answers.yahoo.com/question/index;_ylt=Ama1xMkFwP8ElHWl5gNHgHEjzKIX;_ylv=3?qid=20060721002757AAhZBKu.
24. DesperateWoman, "Hysterectomy Reviews," Daily Strength, July 2008. www.dailystrength.org/treatments/Hysterectomy/page-2.
25. Rena, "My Story."
26. Marcy, "My Story," Eyes on the Prize, August 2000. www.eyesontheprize.org/stories/marcy.html.
27. Leslie S., "My Story," Eyes on the Prize, April 2002. www.eyesontheprize.org/stories/leslies.html.

Chapter Five: Preventing Cervical Cancer

28. World Health Organization, *Comprehensive Cervical Cancer Control: A Guide to Essential Practice*. Geneva, Switzerland: WHO Press, 2006, p. 3.
29. Susan, "Cervical Cancer Survivor: I Made It Through Cervical Cancer Treatment."
30. Craig L. Bissinger, "Pap Smears and Cervical Cancer: What Every Woman Should Know," essortment, August 20, 2002. www.essortment.com/articles/papsmears_100024.htm.
31. Quoted in Claire Cain Miller, "The Cancer That Shouldn't Be," *Forbes*, January 28, 2008, p. 60.

32. Quoted in Donald G. McNeil Jr., "DNA Test Outperforms Pap Smear," *New York Times*, April 7, 2009. www.nytimes.com.

33. Mark Schiffman and Sholom Wacholder, "From India to the World—a Better Way to Prevent Cervical Cancer," *New England Journal of Medicine*, April 2, 2009, p. 1,453.

34. Quoted in McNeil, "DNA Test Outperforms Pap Smear."

35. Quoted in McNeil, "DNA Test Outperforms Pap Smear."

36. National Cancer Institute Factsheet, "Human Papillomavirus (HPV) Vaccines: Questions and Answers," National Cancer Institute, August 12, 2007. www.cancer.gov/cancertopics/factsheet/Prevention/HPV-vaccine.

37. Shannon, "Real-Life Stories," Gardasil Vaccine Information, 2009. www.gardasil.com/gardasil-information/i-chose/index.html.

38. Meg, comment on posting by PalMD, "Gardasil Is a Good Idea," on Denialism Blog, March 31, 2008. http://scienceblogs.com/denialism/2008/03/gardasil_is_a_good_idea.php.

39. DuWayne, comment on posting by PalMD, "Gardasil Is a Good Idea," on Denialism Blog, March 31, 2008. http://scienceblogs.com/denialism/2008/03/gardasil_is_a_good_idea.php.

Chapter Six: Challenges to Overcome

40. Quoted in Associated Press, "Death from Cervical Cancer Easily Preventable," msnbc, August 3, 2005. www.msnbc.msn.com/id/8702775.

41. Krishnan, *The HPV Vaccine Controversy*, p. 175.

42. Quoted in Alliance for Cervical Cancer Prevention, *Women's Stories, Women's Lives: Experiences with Cervical Cancer Screening and Treatment*. Seattle, WA: ACCP, 2004, p. 10.

43. Quoted in Alliance for Cervical Cancer Prevention, *Women's Stories, Women's Lives*, p. 23.

44. Krishnan, *The HPV Vaccine Controversy*, p. 69.

45. fantab27, comment on article "More than a Quarter of O.C. Girls Get Gardasil Vaccine," *OCRegister Online*, February 19, 2009. http://healthyliving.freedomblogging.com/2009/02/19/more-than-a-quarter-of-oc-girls-get-gardasil-vaccine/3163.

46. ses, comment on article "More than a Quarter of O.C. Girls Get Gardasil Vaccine," *OCRegister Online*, February 19, 2009. http://healthyliving.freedomblogging.com/2009/02/19/more-than-a-quarter-of-oc-girls-get-gardasil-vaccine/3163.

47. Quoted in Deborah Kotz, "Gardasil Is Found Safe—but Some Families Wonder," *U.S. News & World Report*, October 24, 2008. www.usnews.com/health/blogs/on-women/2008/10/ 24/gardasil-is-found-safe--but-some-families-wonder.html.

48. Quoted in Pam Belluck, "In New Hampshire, Soft Sell Eases Vaccine Fears," *New York Times*, May 12, 2007. www.nytimes.com/2007/05/12/health/12cancer.html?_r=1.

49. Philadelphia Church of God, "Protecting Our Children—Preventing HPV," *Trumpet*, March 9, 2007. http://thetrumpet.com/index.php?page=article&id=3015.

50. Beki Benning, "Parental Prerogative," Mad as Hell Club, April 9, 2007. www.madashellclub.net/?p=805.

Glossary

adenocarcinoma: Cancer that originates in the cervix's columnar cells.

basement membrane: The bottom layer of the cervical epithelium. This membrane separates the epithelium from the deeper tissues of the cervix.

benign: Not invasive; of no danger to a person's overall health.

Bethesda System: A diagnostic scale that standardizes Pap results by sorting them into categories based on laboratory analysis.

cancer: A disorder in which a group of cells displays uncontrolled growth and invasion of nearby or distant tissues.

carcinoma in situ (CIS): Severe dysplasia that has the potential to become cancerous if not removed.

cervical dysplasia: A condition characterized by disrupted or abnormal growth of cervical epithelial cells.

cervical intraepithelial neoplasia (CIN): *See* cervical dysplasia.

chemotherapy: A procedure in which cancer-killing chemicals are introduced into a patient's bloodstream.

colposcope: An instrument that magnifies the skin of the vagina and cervix, allowing close visual examination of these areas.

colposcopy: A visual exam of the cervix and/or vagina performed with the help of a colposcope.

columnar epithelial cells: Tall, thin cells that make up the epithelium of the endocervical canal.

computed tomography (CT) scan: A procedure that uses X-rays and computers to produce digital images of a patient's body.

conization: A procedure in which a cone-shaped sample of the tissue surrounding the endocervical canal is removed.

cryotherapy: A procedure in which abnormal cells are killed by freezing.

cytopathologist: An expert in the study of diseased cells.

cytoscopy: Visual examination of the urethra and bladder with an instrument called a cytoscope.

ectocervix: The portion of the cervix that extends into the vagina.

endocervical canal: The passage that leads through the cervix, connecting the vagina and the uterine cavity.

endocervical curettage (ECC): A procedure in which cells are scraped off the surface of the endocervical canal.

epithelial cells: The cells that make up the epithelium.

epithelium: Membranous tissue that covers most of the body's internal and external surfaces, including the cervix.

external os: The central opening of the ectocervix.

human papillomaviruses (HPVs): A group of viruses that commonly infect humans. HPVs are known to cause warts and some types of cancer, including cervical cancer.

Hybrid Capture II: A test that detects the DNA of certain high-risk HPVs.

hysterectomy: The surgical removal of a woman's cervix and uterus.

internal os: The opening between the cervix and the uterine cavity.

invasive carcinoma: Cancer that has invaded the surrounding tissues.

keratin: A tough protein that hardens hair, nails, and some other cells of the human body, including cervical squamous cells.

loop electrosurgical excision procedure (LEEP): A procedure in which a heated wire is used to shave tissue off the cervix.

magnetic resonance imaging (MRI) scan: A procedure that uses magnetic energy and radio waves to create digital cross-sections of organs or other body parts.

malignancy: An abnormal growth that tends to invade surrounding tissues.

margins: The edges of a tissue sample removed for lab examination.

metastasis: The movement of cancerous cells from their original site to distant locations in the body, usually via the bloodstream or the lymphatic system.

microinvasion: Microscopic advance of cancerous cells into adjacent tissues.

oncogenic: Having the ability or potential to cause cancer.

Pap test: A procedure in which a doctor scrapes cells from the cervix to check for abnormalities, including cervical dysplasia and cancer.

pelvic lymphadenectomy: The surgical removal of the pelvic lymph nodes.

positron emission tomography (PET) scan: A procedure that uses radioactive chemicals to capture three-dimensional images of a patient's body processes.

proctoscopy: Visual examination of the rectum and lower colon with an instrument called a proctoscope.

prognosis: The predicted course or outcome of a disease.

punch biopsy: A procedure that removes a small chunk of flesh for laboratory examination.

radiation therapy: A procedure during which cancerous cells are killed through exposure to radioactive waves.

radical hysterectomy: The surgical removal of a woman's cervix and uterus along with some lymph nodes, ligaments, and the upper part of the vagina.

radical trachelectomy: The surgical removal of a woman's cervix and upper vagina and the subsequent reattachment of the remaining vagina and uterus.

radiologist: A doctor who specializes in the usage of radiant energy procedures, such as x-ray, and who is trained to interpret the images they produce.

speculum: An instrument that separates the walls of the vagina.

squamous cell carcinoma: Cancer that originates in the cervix's squamous cells.

squamous epithelial cells: Flattened cells that make up the epithelium of the ectocervix.

stage: The severity of a cancer based on its location, size, routes of spread, and other factors.

transformation zone (TZ): The cervical region where columnar cells give way to squamous cells.

urography: A procedure that produces X-ray images of a patient's urinary system.

vaccine: A harmless substance that stimulates an immune response to a specific disease when introduced into a person's body.

Organizations to Contact

American Cancer Society, Inc.
250 Williams St. NW, Ste. 600
Atlanta, GA 30303
phone: (800) ACS-2345
Web site: www.cancer.org

The American Cancer Society is a health organization dedicated to eliminating cancer as a major health problem. Through research, education, advocacy, and service, it seeks to prevent cancer, save lives, and diminish suffering. It offers authoritative information about every type of cancer, including cervical cancer.

Centers for Disease Control and Prevention (CDC)
1600 Clifton Rd.
Atlanta, GA 30333
phone: (404) 639-3311
Web site: www.cdc.gov

The CDC is one of the thirteen major operating components of the U.S. Department of Health and Human Services. As one of the world's top research labs, it plays a major role in researching and taking action against cervical cancer and other disorders.

National Cervical Cancer Coalition (NCCC)
6520 Platt Ave. #693
West Hills, CA 91307
phone: (800) 685-5531
fax: (818) 780-8199
Web site: www.nccc-online.org

Founded in 1996, the NCCC is a coalition of people battling cervical cancer and HPV-related issues. The organization's emphasis is outreach and education for HPV and cervical cancer victims and their families.

World Health Organization (WHO)
Avenue Appia 20
CH-1211 Geneva 27
Switzerland
phone: 41-22-791-2111
fax: 41-22-791-3111
Web site: www.who.int

A part of the United Nations, the WHO works to help people achieve physical, mental, and social well-being. The WHO'S Web site contains current information on diseases and disorders affecting people all over the world.

For More Information

Books

Kris Carr, *Crazy Sexy Cancer Tips*. Guilford, CT: skirt! 2007. Diagnosed with liver cancer at age thirty-one, the author has compiled her experiences into an unforgettable memoir and guidebook for young cancer victims.

Don S. Dizon, *100 Questions & Answers About Cervical Cancer*. Sudbury, MA: Jones & Bartlett, 2008. This book offers both patients' and doctors' views on the issues surrounding cervical cancer, from the most basic medical questions to emotional management and more.

Shobha S. Krishnan, *The HPV Vaccine Controversy: Sex, Cancer, God, and Politics: A Guide for Parents, Women, Men, and Teenagers*. Westport, CT: Praeger, 2008. This book offers a thorough description of HPV and its effects, along with an in-depth look at the issues surrounding HPV vaccination.

Adina Nack, *Damaged Goods? Women Living with Incurable Sexually Transmitted Diseases*. Philadelphia, PA: Temple University Press, 2008. In this book, the author examines the psychological effects of herpes and HPV infection.

Lynda Rushing, *Abnormal Pap Smears: What Every Woman Needs to Know*. Amherst, NY: Prometheus, 2008. This book offers an in-depth look at Pap testing and its many possible results.

Jane Semple, *HPV and Cervical Dysplasia: A Naturopathic Approach*. Salt Lake City, UT: Woodland, 2007. This booklet offers a holistic approach to HPV control, including dietary tips, detoxification strategies, and other suggestions for the natural management of HPV.

Web Sites

Centers for Disease Control (www.cdc.gov). This is the official site of the CDC. Search for "cervical cancer" and "HPV" to uncover a wealth of information about human papillomavirus and the disorders it causes.

National Cancer Institute (www.cancer.gov). A division of the U.S. National Institutes of Health, this site is a gateway for information about every aspect of cervical cancer. It offers basic facts, screening guidelines, HPV vaccination summaries, clinical trial searches, and much more.

World Health Organization (www.who.int). Like the CDC Web site, the WHO Web site contains a great deal of information on cervical cancer and HPV. It includes a searchable database of world cancer statistics.

Index

Picture Credits

About the Author

Kris Hirschmann has written more than two hundred books for children. She owns and runs The Wordshop (www.the-wordshop.com), a business that provides a variety of writing and editorial services. She holds a bachelor's degree in psychology from Dartmouth College in Hanover, New Hampshire.

Hirschmann lives just outside Orlando, Florida, with her husband, Michael, and her daughters, Nikki and Erika.